Careers for You Series

CAREERS FOR

EXTROVERTS

& Other Gregarious Types

JAN GOLDBERG

SECOND EDITION

McGraw·Hill

New York   Chicago   San Francisco   Lisbon   London   Madrid   Mexico City
Milan   New Delhi   San Juan   Seoul   Singapore   Sydney   Toronto .

The *McGraw·Hill* Companies

Library of Congress Cataloging-in-Publication Data

Goldberg, Jan.
      Careers for extroverts & other gregarious types / by Jan Goldberg — 2nd ed.
         p.   cm.   —   (McGraw-Hill careers for you series)
      ISBN 0-07-144860-8 (alk. paper)
         1. Vocational guidance—United States.   2. Extroversion.   I. Title: Careers
for extroverts and other gregarious types.   II. Title.   III. Series.

HF5381.G5682 2006
331.702—dc22   2005004080

· ·

This book is dedicated to the memory of
my beloved parents, Sam and Sylvia
Lefkovitz, and the memory of a dear
uncle, Bernard Lefko.

2 3 4 5 6 7 8 9 0   DOC/DOC   0 9 8 7 6

ISBN 0-07-144860-8

McGraw-Hill books are available at special quantity discounts to use as premiums and
sales promotions, or for use in corporate training programs. For more information,
please write to the Director of Special Sales, Professional Publishing, McGraw-Hill,
Two Penn Plaza, New York, NY 10121-2298. Or contact your local bookstore.

This book is printed on acid-free paper.

Contents

Acknowledgments

The author gratefully acknowledges the numerous professionals who graciously agreed to be profiled in this book and the following:

- My dear husband, Larry, for his inspiration and vision
- My children—Sherri, Deborah, and Bruce—for their encouragement and love
- Family and close friends—Adrienne, Marty, Mindi, Cary, Michele, Paul, Michele, Alison, Steve, Marci, Steve, Brian, Steven, Jesse, Bertha, and Aunt Helen—for their faith and support
- Diana Catlin, for her insights and input

The editors would like to thank Josephine Scanlon for revising this second edition.

Attention: Extroverts

Man absolutely cannot live by himself.
—Erich Fromm

In everyday language, the word *extrovert* refers to a sociable person who makes friends easily. The Swiss psychologist Carl G. Jung gave it a more technical definition by saying that extroversion meant "turning the interests and energies of the mind towards events, people and things of the outer world." In other words, extroverts are likely to be more focused on whatever is going on around them than on their own thoughts and feelings.

Are You an Extrovert?

He who lives only for himself is truly dead to others.
—Publilius Syrus

Are you the kind of person who looks outside yourself? Do you want to follow a career that allows you to interact with others? If you're not sure, take the following quiz and you'll find out.

EXTROVERT QUIZ
1. Do you usually enjoy a good rapport with others?
2. Do you have a sincere desire to please others?
3. Do you enjoy working in groups?

4. Do you like the idea of working with others for the common good?
5. Would you rather work in a crowded office than in an isolated lab?
6. Does it bother you if you are cut off from dealing with people?
7. Do you find it easy to relate to a variety of people—even if you don't know them?
8. Do you feel rewarded when others are enriched by your actions?
9. Do you adapt easily to a flexible schedule, one that might include more than forty hours per week and nights and/or weekends?
10. Are you able to travel if necessary?
11. Are you willing to attend seminars and workshops and practice other means of keeping your skills sharp?

This book explores the following careers as some of the occupations that extroverts would do well to consider: careers in acting, music and dance, sales, politics, marketing and advertising, and public relations and fund-raising. Though these are, by no means, the only possibilities for extroverts, they afford you a long list of careers to consider.

A man wrapped up in himself makes a very small bundle.
—Benjamin Franklin

CHAPTER ONE

Careers in Acting

Attempt the impossible in order to improve your work.
—Bette Davis

D o you enjoy being in the spotlight, providing enjoyment for others? Actors do. The world of acting includes a multitude of possibilities for those who like to perform.

Defining What Actors Do

Whether portraying someone young or old, dramatic or comedic, actors bring their characters to life using voices, gestures, and movements. By definition, actors perform in stage, radio, television, video, or motion-picture productions. They also work in cabarets, nightclubs, theme parks, commercials, and industrial films produced for training and educational purposes.

Though acting is often viewed as a glamorous profession, the truth is that many actors are forced to put in long and irregular hours (including rehearsals and performances) with little payment in return. Most actors struggle to find steady work; only a few ever achieve recognition as stars. Some well-known, experienced performers may be cast in supporting roles. Others work as extras, with no lines to deliver, or make brief, cameo appearances, speaking only one or two lines. Some actors do voice-over and narration work for advertisements, animated features, books on tape, and other electronic media. They also teach in high school or university drama departments, acting conservatories, or public programs.

Qualifications and Training for Actors

Experienced actors recommend that those who hope to pursue this career gain experience by taking part in high school and college productions. In addition, performing in local community theater provides an opportunity for aspiring actors to hone their skills. Public high schools dedicated to education in the performing arts can be found in many cities throughout the United States and Canada.

Formal dramatic training, either through an acting conservatory or a university program, generally is necessary to enter the profession; however, some people successfully enter the field without it. Most people studying for a bachelor's degree take courses in radio and television broadcasting, communications, film, theater, drama, or dramatic literature. Many continue their academic training to earn a master of fine arts (M.F.A.) degree. Advanced curricula may include courses in stage speech and movement, directing, playwriting, and design, as well as intensive acting workshops. The National Association of Schools of Theatre accredits 128 programs in theater arts.

Many actors, regardless of experience level, pursue continued training through acting conservatories or by working with a drama coach. Actors also research roles so that they can grasp concepts quickly during rehearsals and understand the story's setting and background. Sometimes actors learn a foreign language or train with a dialect coach to develop an accent to make their characters more realistic.

Desirable Traits for Actors

Among the most desirable personal traits for actors are creative instincts, innate talent, and the intellectual ability to perform.

Actors should be passionate about performing and truly enjoy entertaining others. In addition, determination, perseverance, and a good memory also enhance an actor's ability to win roles.

Actors must have poise, stage presence, and the ability to affect an audience. They must also be able to follow direction. Since physical appearance can definitely be a deciding factor in being selected for particular roles, actors should be able and willing to adopt different looks when pursuing new roles. Actors also need stamina to withstand the heat of stage or studio lights; heavy costumes; the long, irregular hours; and the adverse weather conditions that may exist on location.

Building a Career

The best way to start building an acting career is to pursue local opportunities and move on from there to larger prospects. Basic experience can be acquired through modeling, acting groups, and local and regional theater. Any or all of these may help in obtaining work in the major entertainment markets—New York and Los Angeles.

Most actors list with casting agencies that help them find parts. Many take advantage of the services offered by the unions listed at the end of this chapter. Many professional actors rely on agents or managers to find work, negotiate contracts, and plan their careers. Agents generally earn a percentage of an actor's contract.

As actors' reputations grow, they work on larger productions or in more prestigious theaters. Actors also advance to lead or specialized roles. A few actors move into acting-related jobs as drama coaches or directors of stage, television, radio, or motion-picture productions. Some teach drama in colleges and universities.

The length of a performer's working life depends largely on training, skill, versatility, and perseverance. Some actors continue working throughout their lives; however, large numbers also leave the occupation after a short time because they cannot find enough work to make a living.

Extra! Extra! Read All About It!

In addition to the actors with speaking parts, extras, who have small parts with no lines to deliver, are used throughout the industry. To become a movie extra (also known as a background artist), one must usually be listed with a casting agency, such as Central Casting, a no-fee agency that supplies all extras to the major movie studios in Hollywood.

Acting Strategies: Finding a Job

Armed with your college degree, basic knowledge of the acting business, and some experience, you'll need to prepare a portfolio that highlights your qualifications, acting history, and special skills. The portfolio should include a resume along with photos, or head shots, taken by a professional photographer whom you trust to show you off to your best advantage. Attach your resume to the back of your picture with staples at the upper left- and right-hand corners.

Once your portfolio is complete, you can start making the rounds of casting offices, ad agencies, producers' offices, and agents. Several trade publications contain casting information, ads for part-time jobs, information about shows, and other pertinent data about what's going on in the industry. Among these are *Back Stage* and the weekly *Variety* in New York and Los Angeles and *Ross Reports* in New York. In Los Angeles, there's also *Daily Variety* and *Hollywood Reporter*. You can find all of these, as well as other information about casting calls and acting opportunities, on the Internet.

Once you drop off your resume and head shots, you certainly shouldn't just wait for the phone to ring. Stay active by remaining in contact—it may even be a good idea to drop by the various offices and say hello. Be sure to check in by phone every week to see if any opportunities are available for you. If you are currently in a show, send prospective employers a flyer. This shows them that you are a working actor.

Audition Tips

When you get past this initial stage and actually win an audition, here are some points to remember:

1. Be prepared.
2. Be familiar with the piece—read it beforehand and choose the parts you'd like to try out for.
3. Go for it—don't hold back.
4. Speak loudly and clearly—project your voice to the back of the room.
5. Take chances.
6. Try not to be the one going first—if you can. Observe others so that you can pick up on what the evaluators seem to like or dislike.
7. Be enthusiastic and confident.
8. Keep auditioning—even if you don't get parts, you are getting invaluable experience that is bound to pay off at some point.

When Do You Need an Agent?

The answer: not right away. You don't need an agent to audition for everything, and there are many roles you can audition for that do not require an agent, such as theater or films. However, most commercials are cast through agencies, so you would most likely need an agent to land one.

Compensation

While waiting to be chosen for a part, many acting hopefuls take jobs as waiters, bartenders, taxi drivers, and so on, working at jobs that allow for a flexible schedule and some money to live on.

Minimum salaries, hours of work, and other conditions of employment for professional actors are covered in collective bargaining agreements between producers of shows and unions representing workers. The Actors' Equity Association represents stage actors; the Screen Actors Guild (SAG) and the Screen Extras Guild cover those working in motion pictures, including television, commercials, and films; and the American Federation of Television and Radio Artists (AFTRA) represents television and radio performers. While these unions generally determine minimum salaries, any actor or director may negotiate for a salary higher than the minimum.

Under terms of a joint SAG and AFTRA contract covering all unionized workers, motion-picture and television actors with speaking parts earned a minimum daily rate of $678 or $2,352 for a five-day week in 2003. Actors also receive contributions to their health and pension plans and additional compensation for reruns and foreign telecasts of the productions in which they appear.

According to Equity, the minimum weekly salary for actors in Broadway productions in 2003 was $1,354. Actors working in Off-Broadway theaters received minimums ranging from $479 to $557 a week, depending on the seating capacity of the theater. Regional theaters that operate under an Equity agreement pay actors $531 to $800 per week. For touring productions, actors receive an additional $111 per day for living expenses ($117 per day in larger, higher-cost cities).

Some well-known actors earn well above the minimum; their salaries are many times the figures cited, creating the false impression that all actors are highly paid. For example, of the nearly one hundred thousand SAG members, only about fifty might be considered stars. The average income that SAG members earn from acting—less than $5,000 a year—is low because employment is erratic. Therefore, most actors must supplement their incomes by holding jobs in other occupations.

Many actors who work more than a set number of weeks per year are covered by a union health, welfare, and pension fund that includes hospitalization insurance and to which employers contribute. Under some employment conditions, Equity and AFTRA members receive paid vacations and sick leave.

Words from the Pros

Following are the personal accounts of five professional actors. Read their stories to see whether this career might be right for you.

Jennifer Aquino, Actor

Jennifer Aquino has appeared in television, movies, and stage productions. Her credits include the television shows "Weird Science," "Caroline in the City," "JAG," and "Twin Peaks." Jennifer's movie credits include *The Party Crashers*, *Prisoners of Love*, *Screenland Drive*, and *Ralph the Waiter*. She has performed on stage in *People Like Me* at the Playwrights' Arena, *Gila River* at Japan America Theater, and *Cabaret* and *Sophisticated Barflies* at East West Players. These are only a few of her accomplishments.

Jennifer is the lead voice of Catherine Stanfield in Microsoft and Genki's Xbox car chasing combat game "Maximum Chase" and is the recurring voice of Chelsea in the new Rugrats animated series "All Grown Up." You can also see her in a national commercial for Home Depot.

Jennifer enjoyed performing for her family as a child and acted for the first time in elementary school. She received the Performing Arts Award in high school and ultimately studied theater and dance at UCLA while earning a B.A. in economics. Her first break after graduation was playing a character in the television series "Twin Peaks," a job she won after her very first audition. Jennifer then got an agent and joined the Screen Actors Guild and continues performing in theatrical productions. She is a founding member of Theater West and the East West Players Network.

Like most actors starting their careers, Jennifer initially held a full-time job while pursuing her dream. She worked in the health care industry for Kaiser Foundation Health Plan and then as a health care consultant for the accounting firm Deloitte & Touche. Jennifer was fortunate since, as she says, "I was such a good employee that my managers would be flexible and let me go out on auditions. After a few years, I realized that I was working too many hours (seventy to eighty per week), and I finally had to make a decision to quit my day job and focus 100 percent of my time toward acting. After booking a few jobs, including a national commercial, I was able to do so. It was a big risk, but one I felt was necessary to take. I remember what my acting coach would say— 'part-time work gets part-time results.' The more I put into acting, the more I got out of it."

As a full-time actor, Jennifer still maintains a very busy schedule. She works forty to sixty hours each week, either preparing for an upcoming job or audition or interacting with agents and managers and promoting herself to casting directors, producers, and writers. Jennifer is aware of the stress that can result from such a busy schedule and also works hard at maintaining her health and having some time to relax.

Jennifer talks about the ups and downs of acting: "What I like most about my work is that I can say that I am making a living doing what I absolutely love to do, and that I am pursuing my passion in life. Not too many people in this world can say that. What I like least about my work is that there are a lot of politics in it. It's not always the best actor who gets the job. Some of the time it's a certain look, what your credits are, who you know, and so forth, that determines who gets the job. There are a lot of things that are out of your control. That's just part of the business and you have to accept it."

Gonzo Schexnayder, Actor

Gonzo Schexnayder is an actor following a different path from Jennifer's. He has a B.A. in journalism and advertising from Louisiana State University in Baton Rouge and has taken acting classes at LSU and Monterey Peninsula College in California. In addition, he has attended Chicago's Second City Training Center and the Actors Center. Gonzo is also a member of both SAG and AFTRA.

Gonzo's initial dream was to do stand-up comedy, but he did not pursue it until he graduated from college and began working with an improvisational comedy group. Within a few months he was on military assignment in Monterey, California, for language training. During this time Gonzo had his first show, and he still recalls how happy the experience made him: "I'd never felt such elation as when I performed. Nothing in my life had given me the sheer thrill and rush that I experienced by creating a character and maintaining that throughout a given period of time. Nothing else mattered but that moment on stage, my other actors, and the scene we were performing."

Realizing how important it was for him to be happy with his work, Gonzo decided to pursue acting as his career. Although this meant developing his acting while also working at a more steady job, Gonzo was willing to make the commitment. As he says, "Sure, I'd love to have an apartment with central air and a balcony. I'd love to have a car that is still under warranty. But I know that by putting my efforts and money into my acting career, those other things don't matter. . . . Cars and apartments don't give me the satisfaction that being an actor does."

Gonzo's schedule varies depending on the project he is involved in. He is a founding member of Broad Shoulders Theatre in Chicago, which takes a good deal of his time. He is also pursuing a voice-over/on-camera career and attends classes and workshops toward that end.

Gonzo offers his views on the ups and downs of acting: "I love the process of acting and sometimes just the fast-paced, eclectic nature of the business. There is always something new to learn and something new to try. The sheer excitement of performing live is amazing, and the personal satisfaction of getting an audience to laugh or cry simply by your words and actions is very gratifying.

"I dislike pretentious actors and people who take advantage of an actor's desire to perform. As one of the only professions where there is an abundance of people willing to work for nothing, producers, casting directors, agents, and managers who only care about the money will take advantage of and abuse actors for personal gain. Being an astute actor helps prevent much of this, but one must always be on the lookout."

Jack Stauffer, Actor

Jack Stauffer, a graduate of Northwestern University, has been a working actor since 1968. He created the role of Chuck Tyler in the popular television daytime drama, "All My Children" and remained in that role for three and a half years—a total of 386 shows. Other regular television appearances include "Battlestar Galactica" and "The Young and the Restless." Episodic television appearances include "Lois and Clark," "Viper," "Designing Women," "Quantum Leap," "Perfect Strangers," "Growing Pains," "Knots Landing," and "Dynasty." In all, he has appeared in forty prime-time television shows and numerous movies of the week and miniseries. He was also costar of the movie *Chattanooga Choo Choo*. In theater, he had parts in *My Fair Lady* and *Oliver* at the Grove Theatre in San Bernardino County. Other play productions include *The Music Man, Annie Get Your Gun, Fiorello, Can Can, Mister Roberts*, and *Guys and Dolls*. His list of achievements also includes parts in more than two hundred commercials.

"I started as a child actor but really didn't become a professional until I graduated from college in 1968," says Stauffer. "I simply sold my car, moved to New York, and hit the pavement!"

Jack Stauffer basically grew up in the entertainment industry. His mother worked for Warner Brothers and was W.C. Fields's radio producer. His father also worked as a radio producer and started his own advertising agency, which was responsible for many early television shows. Jack was accustomed to being around celebrities and had wanted to join the ranks of performers since his childhood.

Jack is honest about the reality of working as an actor. As he says, "Unless you are on a series or are a celebrity, you are constantly battling the belief that you will probably never work again. Thus, your workday consists of looking everywhere and calling anyone who might give you a job. Once you have done all you can do, you inevitably wait for the phone to ring. The vast majority of the time, it doesn't. So, most actors have other jobs— temporary work or selling or, in my case, teaching tennis—anything to make enough money to pay the bills so you can pursue your craft. When you are finally hired for a day or a week or a month or whatever it might be, every moment in your day suddenly has purpose. You get to do what you were meant to do, even if it is only for a short time or if the part is minuscule. You are on top of the world. Then it is over, and it is back to square one."

For Jack, the work is its own reward, and he believes that this feeling is shared by most actors who are dedicated to their craft. "The best thing about your work is the work itself," he says. "An actor lives by his emotions and his ability to convey them to an audience. A good actor makes it look easy even though it is very hard. This partially explains why so many actors are willing to work for free. It is the work that fulfills them. Of course, if you get paid, it is much better. The recognition factor is important also. That is why so many actors return to the stage. The gratification is immediate. Any actor who says the applause means nothing to him is probably lying."

Jack also discusses the negative side of his profession. "The worst thing about the industry is that absolute lack of tenure. You are only as good as your next job. Your history, experience, and so on, don't mean much because there is no studio system anymore. With no continuity, it is difficult to slowly work your way up the ladder of success. The easiest way to get hired today is to have the executive producer of a hit show as your brother-in-law."

Jack Stauffer offers some candid advice for anyone considering a career in acting. "If you have an absolute, undying, uncontrollable passion to do this—and I mean you will die if you don't— then by all means give it everything you've got. But if you are the slightest bit timid or unsure, choose another career. This is a business based on rejection, and it can destroy you. If you sell cars and somebody doesn't buy one, they simply don't want that car. As an actor, when you are turned down, they don't want you. It's difficult not to take it personally. You have to be very strong to keep at it."

Joseph Bowman, Actor

Joseph Bowman is an actor in the Los Angeles area who considers himself at the beginning stage of his career. A high school graduate, he has some college, vocational, and military training and has also participated in the Vanguard Theatre Ensemble Training.

While it might seem an unlikely background for an actor, six years in the Marine Corps actually reinforced Joseph's love of performing. "I thoroughly loved the United States military," he says. "It tended to reward a person who acted as if he enjoyed this kind of life, and I was such a person. It seems that I have always been able to act appropriately in any given situation. Older people usually find me charming. Younger people usually find me cool. I love to be the chameleon."

Following his military service, Joseph took part in a model/talent showcase. Although the production itself was not a great success, the experience rekindled his love of performing.

Joseph currently does what he calls background work. His military experience gets him work in productions that want people with actual experience for certain roles. Much of this work involves firing military weapons (blanks) and an awareness of related safety issues.

In describing his job, Joseph says, "There are not many typical days in acting because every production is very different. It is like working for a different company in a different capacity every day. I may be asked to simply put on a costume and chat (mime) with another actor for eight hours one day. Another day, I might be asked to put on the full battle dress uniform of a branch of the military and fire an M-16 at a monster that isn't there! It varies widely, and that is why I love it.

"The hours and working conditions also vary greatly. Typically, jobs consist of ten-hour days with pleasant working conditions. Sometimes a 'shoot' can be as quick as three hours, and sometimes it takes thirteen. It all depends on what the director is looking for and when he or she sees it."

Joseph greatly enjoys being involved in the arts and having the opportunity to interact with other artists. "I most enjoy the variety and the opportunity to become a character," he says. "I have worked my share of day jobs, and I hated the monotony of them. Fame is not my goal. Riches are not my goal. I simply want to do what I love and get paid for it. That is my dream.

"The only thing I don't like about acting is that there is a lot of classism. If you are on a 'shoot' as a background actor, many do not afford you the level of treatment that featured or lead actors enjoy. It is simply a fact of life. Most actors at a high level do not act snobbish to the lowest-rung actors, but many of the production people do."

Joseph Bowman offers some practical advice about preparing for an acting career. "I would advise those interested in this field to study the craft and art of acting as if your life depended upon it. Enjoy life and experience it to the fullest because good artists bring all their life experiences to their art. And don't let anyone tell you that you are a fool for following your dream. In your later years, would you rather look back and say, 'I wish I had at least tried' or 'I gave it my best shot and had fun along the way'?"

Joe Hansard, Actor and Stand-Up Comedian

Auditioning for a television commercial at the age of five was enough for Joe Hansard to become hooked, and he currently works as an actor and a stand-up comedian in New York City. He attended trade school at the Broadcasting Institute of Maryland and has also been an actor in residence at the International Film

& Television Workshops. Other training includes Stand-Up New York (comedian school) and the Mike Fenton Scene Study Workshop for Film. He has performed his comedy routine at several comedy clubs in New York, and his favorite acting credit is the part of Jimmy Lee Shields in the pilot episode of NBC's "Homicide."

Joe has also completed the feature film *Brainiac* (the sequel), to be released in 2005. Other feature film credits include *Thread*, *Soulmates*, and *The Hitter*. He has also had lead or featured roles in nearly twenty independent short films and has appeared in several corporate videos.

"I've always had a fascination for the motion picture industry," Joe says. "I enjoy the camaraderie and collaboration that comes with a film or television project, as well as the challenges. I liken it to being in a football game, where you are given the ball and you run with it. As an actor, I try to expand on the ideas given me by bringing my own uniqueness to a role.

"Since there is nothing better than working with folks who truly love their work and get excited about what they do, I like surrounding myself with creative, enthusiastic, and energetic people. As a stand-up comedian, nothing is more exhilarating than laughter and applause. It is sweeter than any candy, and it doesn't rot my teeth!"

Joe credits his parents with supporting his aspirations. He performed at talent shows in elementary school and began doing magic tricks in his early teens. After high school, he was uncertain about his career plans, and his mother suggested a trade school for broadcasting. Joe's first job was as a DJ for an AM radio station in Shippensburg, Pennsylvania. He eventually joined the Screen Actors Guild when director Christopher Leitch cast him in a principal role in the feature film *The Hitter*, starring Ron O'Neal and Adolph Caesar.

Establishing an acting career can be very difficult, and Joe is honest about his early struggles. "I moved to Los Angeles in the early 1980s and had an absolutely horrible experience there," he says. "I couldn't get work, had my car repossessed, went bankrupt, and was in poor shape emotionally. It was the darkest time of my life, and there seemed to be no light at the end of the tunnel. But I finally got my act together and moved back east, and that's when Barry Levinson cast me in the pilot episode of 'Homicide' on NBC. The 'Gone for Goode' episode in which I appear aired after the Super Bowl in 1993 and was the highest-rated 'Homicide' episode ever."

Following this break, Joe decided to pursue stand-up comedy as a way of getting exposure. He was a finalist in HBO's Aspen Comedy Festival 2000 northeast regional competition at the Improv. He has also performed at Caroline's, Gotham Comedy Club, Stand-Up New York, and Don't Tell Mama (New York); Atlantis Theater (Toronto); the Improv, Headliners Comedy Club, the Fun Factory, Lewie's, Champions, Wiseacres, and Winchesters (D.C. and Baltimore); and the Comedy Store (Hollywood).

Like most actors, Joe spends a good deal of time looking for work. He tracks casting leads through personal contacts with industry professionals, on the Internet, and through word of mouth. "This is a crazy business," Joe says. "Sometimes it's busy and full beyond belief and there's barely time to catch my breath. At other times, weeks and even months go by with nary a job in sight."

Joe's schedule when he is filming a movie or television show generally consists of long days, between ten and fourteen hours. While the work is usually enjoyable, the potential exists for less than pleasant conditions. As Joe says, "There is either a real camaraderie that forms on a set or a real paranoia, depending on any number of circumstances and variables in or out of your control that are inherent to the industry. In most cases, it is quite enjoyable, as cast and crew are very professional, and you, more often than not, will get kudos when the director or producer likes the work you are doing. I've found that the entire production and creative team literally evolves into a family.

"I like to work. I love meeting and working with creative, talented actors and directors. I love the business and wouldn't trade it for anything. But the thing I like least is not having any work, having to sit idle. In any case, I see an acting coach once a week and take classes to stay tuned up.

Joe Hansard has a suggestion for aspiring actors: "I would tell others that the most important thing is to love your work. Know that there is much competition and some lean times, but always remember to enjoy what you do and have fun doing it!"

For More Information

Information about opportunities in regional theaters may be obtained from:

Theatre Communications Group
520 Eighth Avenue, Twenty-Fourth Floor
New York, NY 10018
www.tcg.org

A directory of theatrical programs may be purchased from:

National Association of Schools of Theatre
11250 Roger Bacon Drive, Suite 21
Reston, VA 20190
http://nast.arts-accredit.org

Additional information may be obtained from the following associations:

Actors' Equity Association
165 West Forty-Sixth Street
New York, NY 10036
www.actorsequity.org

Alliance of Canadian Cinema, Television, and Radio Artists
   (ACTRA)
625 Church Street, Third Floor
Toronto, ON M4Y 2G1
Canada
www.actra.com

Alliance of Resident Theaters/New York
575 Eighth Avenue, Suite 17 South
New York, NY 10018
www.offbroadwayonline.com

American Association of Community Theatres
8402 BriarWood Crescent
Lago Vista, TX 78645
www.aact.org

American Federation of Television and Radio Artists (AFTRA)
New York National Office
260 Madison Avenue
New York, NY 10016
or
Los Angeles National Office
5757 Wilshire Boulevard, Ninth Floor
Los Angeles, CA 90036
www.aftra.org

American Film Institute
2021 North Western Avenue
Los Angeles, CA 90027
www.afi.com

American Theatre Works
PO Box 510
Dorset, VT 05251
www.theatredirectories.com

Canadian Actors' Equity Association
44 Victoria Street, Twelfth Floor
Toronto, ON M5C 3C4
Canada
www.caea.com

Screen Actors Guild (SAG)
Hollywood Office
5757 Wilshire Boulevard
Los Angeles, CA 90036
or
New York Office
316 Madison Avenue, Twelfth Floor
New York, NY 10017
www.sag.org

CHAPTER TWO

Careers in Music and Dance

Music is edifying, for from time to time it sets the soul in operation.
—John Cage

Arthur Rubinstein learned the names of the piano keys by the time he was two years old. Ray Charles began to play the piano at age three. Yehudi Menuhin performed solos with the San Francisco Symphony Orchestra at the age of seven. Buddy Holly won five dollars singing "Down the River of Memories" at a talent show at age five. Gladys Knight won two thousand dollars singing on Ted Mack's "Original Amateur Hour" at age seven. Marvin Hamlisch was accepted at the Juilliard School of Music when he was seven years old. All of these musical geniuses got their starts very early, as those who choose careers in music and dance often do.

Approximately 215,000 musicians perform in the United States. Included in this number are those who play in any one of thirty-nine regional, ninety metropolitan, or thirty major symphony orchestras. (Large orchestras employ from eighty-five to more than a hundred musicians, while smaller ones employ sixty to seventy-five players.) Also counted are those who perform with small orchestras, symphony orchestras, pop and jazz groups, as well as those who broadcast or record.

Defining What Musicians Do

Instrumental musicians may play a variety of musical instruments in an orchestra, popular band, marching band, military band, concert band, symphony, dance band, rock group, or jazz group and may specialize in string, brass, woodwind, or percussion instruments or electronic synthesizers. A large percentage of musicians are proficient in playing several related instruments, such as the flute and clarinet, which increases their employment opportunities. Some who are very talented have the option to perform as soloists.

Rehearsing and performing take up much of a musician's time and energy. In addition, musicians may need to perform a number of other routine tasks, such as making reservations, keeping track of auditions and/or recordings, arranging for equipment to enhance performances, designing lighting or costuming, doing makeup, handling bookkeeping, and setting up advertising, concerts, tickets, programs, and contracts. This is especially the case for musicians who do not have agents. Musicians also need to plan the sequence of the selections to be performed and/or arrange their music according to the conductor's instructions before performances.

Musicians must keep their instruments clean, polished, tuned, and in proper working order. In addition, they are expected to attend meetings with agents, employers, and conductors or directors to discuss contracts, engagements, and any other business activities.

The Range of Opportunities for Musicians

Performing musicians encompass a wide variety of careers. Here are just a few of the possibilities for musicians and others who love music.

Session Musician

The session musician is responsible for playing background music in a studio while a recording artist is singing. The session musician may also be called a freelance musician, a backup musician, a session player, or a studio musician. Session musicians are used for all kinds of recordings—Broadway musicals, operas, rock and folk songs, and pop tunes.

Versatility is the most important quality for these professionals—the more instruments the musician has mastered, the greater the number of musical styles he or she can offer and, therefore, the more possibilities for musical assignments. Session musicians often are listed through contractors who call upon them when the need arises. Other possibilities exist through direct requests made by the artists themselves, the group members, or the management team.

The ability to sight-read is important for all musicians but it is particularly critical for session musicians. Rehearsal time is usually very limited, and high costs make it too expensive for doing retakes.

Section Member

Section members are the musicians who play instruments in an orchestra. They must be talented at playing their instruments and able to learn the music on their own. Rehearsals are strictly designed for putting all the instruments and individuals together and for establishing cues such as phrasing and correct breathing. It is expected that all musicians practice sufficiently on their own before rehearsals.

Concertmaster

Those chosen to be concertmasters have the important responsibility of leading the string sections of the orchestras during both rehearsals and concerts. In addition, these professionals are responsible for tuning the rest of the orchestra. This is the "music" you hear for about fifteen to twenty seconds before the musicians begin to play the first piece. Concertmasters must possess leadership abilities and be very knowledgeable about both the music and all the instruments. They answer directly to the conductor.

Floor Show Band Member

Musicians who belong to bands that perform floor shows appear in hotels, nightclubs, cruise ships, bars, concert arenas, and cafés. Usually the bands do two shows per night with a particular number of sets in each show. Additionally, they may be required to play one or two dance sets during the course of the engagement. Shows may include costumes, dialogue, singing, jokes, skits, unusual sound effects, and anything else the band decides to include. Floor-show bands may be contracted to appear in one place for one night or for several weeks at a time. As expected, a lot of traveling is involved for those who take up this career.

Announcer or Disc Jockey

Announcers play an important role in keeping listeners tuned in to a radio or television station. They are the ones who must read messages, commercials, and scripts in an entertaining, interesting, and/or enlightening way. They are also responsible for introducing station breaks, and they may interview guests and sell commercial time to advertisers. Disc jockeys are the announcers who oversee musical programming at radio stations and during parties, dances, and other special occasions.

Disc jockeys may also interview guests, make public service announcements, announce the time, do the weather forecast, or even report the news. They must be very knowledgeable about music in general and all aspects of their specialties, specifically the music and the groups who play or sing in that genre of music. Their programs may feature general music, rock, pop, country and western, or any specific musical period or style, such as tunes from the 1950s or 1960s.

Since radio programs are usually performed live, disc jockeys must be quick thinking and personable. Most often they do not have a written script to simply read. They also must be able to perform well under stress and in situations where things do not go as planned. Thus, the best disc jockeys possess pleasant, soothing voices and good wit and are able to keep listeners fully entertained.

It takes considerable skills to work the radio controls, read reports, watch the clock, select music, talk with someone, and be entertaining to the audience—all at the same time.

Conductor and Choral Director

The music conductor is the director for all of the performers in a musical presentation, whether it be singing or instrumental. Though there are many types of conductors—symphony, choral groups, dance bands, opera, marching bands, and ballet—in all cases the music conductor is the one in charge of interpreting the music.

Conductors audition and select musicians, choose the music to accommodate the talents and abilities of the musicians, and direct rehearsals and performances, applying conducting techniques to achieve desired musical effects such as harmony, rhythm, tempo, and shading.

Orchestral conductors lead instrumental music groups, such as orchestras, dance bands, and various popular ensembles. Choral directors are in charge of choirs and glee clubs, sometimes working with a band or orchestra conductor.

Qualifications and Training

Most aspiring musicians begin studying an instrument at an early age. They often gain valuable experience playing in a school or community band or an orchestra or with a group of friends. Singers usually start training when their voices mature. Active participation in school musicals or choirs often provides good early training and experience.

Musicians need extensive and prolonged training to acquire the necessary skills, knowledge, and ability to interpret music. Like other artists, musicians and singers continually strive to stretch themselves by exploring different forms of music. Formal training may be obtained through private study with an accomplished musician, in a college or university music program, or in a music conservatory. An audition is generally necessary for admission to a university or conservatory.

The National Association of Schools of Music accredits nearly six hundred college-level programs in music. Courses typically include music theory, music interpretation, composition, conducting, and performance in a particular instrument or in voice. Music directors, composers, conductors, and arrangers need considerable related work experience or advanced training in these subjects.

Many colleges, universities, and music conservatories grant bachelor's or higher degrees in music. A master's or doctoral degree is usually required to teach advanced music courses in colleges and universities; a bachelor's degree may be sufficient to teach basic courses. A degree in music education qualifies graduates for a state certificate to teach music in public elementary or secondary schools. Musicians who do not meet public school music education requirements may teach in private schools and recreation associations or instruct individual students in private sessions.

Musicians must be knowledgeable about a broad range of musical styles but keenly aware of the form that interests them most. This broader range of interest, knowledge, and training can help expand both employment opportunities and musical abilities. Voice training and private instrumental lessons, especially if taken at an early age, also help develop technique and enhance one's performance.

Advancement for musicians usually means becoming better known and performing for higher earnings. Successful musicians often rely on agents or managers to find them performing engagements, negotiate contracts, and develop their careers.

Desirable Traits for Musicians

Young people considering careers in music should have musical talent, versatility, creativity, poise, and a good stage presence. Because quality performance requires constant study and practice, self-discipline is vital.

In addition, musicians who play in concerts or in nightclubs and those who tour must have physical stamina to endure frequent travel and an irregular performance schedule. Musicians and singers always must make their performances look effortless; therefore, preparation and practice are important. They also must be prepared to face the anxiety of intermittent employment and of rejection when auditioning for work.

Compensation

Earnings for musicians often depend on a performer's professional reputation, place of employment, and the number of hours worked. The most successful musicians can earn far more than the minimum salaries indicated below.

Median annual earnings of salaried musicians and singers were $36,290 in 2002. The middle 50 percent earned between $18,660 and $59,970. The lowest 10 percent earned less than $13,040, and the highest 10 percent earned more than $96,250. Median annual earnings were $43,060 in performing arts companies and $18,160 in religious organizations.

Median annual earnings of salaried music directors and composers were $31,310 in 2002. The middle 50 percent earned between $23,820 and $46,350. The lowest 10 percent earned less than $14,590, and the highest 10 percent earned more than $67,330.

According to the American Federation of Musicians, weekly minimum salaries in major orchestras ranged from $734 to $1,925 during the 2002–03 performing season. Each orchestra works out a separate contract with its local union, with individual musicians eligible to negotiate a higher salary. Top orchestras have a season ranging from twenty-four to fifty-two weeks, with eighteen orchestras reporting fifty-two-week contracts. In regional orchestras, minimum salaries are often less because fewer performances are scheduled. Community orchestras often have yet more limited levels of funding and offer salaries that are much lower for seasons of shorter duration. Regional orchestra musicians often are paid per performance, without any guarantee of future employment.

Although musicians employed by some symphony orchestras work under master wage agreements, which guarantee a season's work up to fifty-two weeks, many other musicians face relatively long periods of unemployment between jobs. Thus, their earnings usually are lower than earnings in many other occupations. Moreover, because they may not work steadily for one employer, some performers cannot qualify for unemployment compensation, and few have typical benefits such as sick leave or paid vacations. For these reasons, many musicians give private lessons or take jobs unrelated to music to supplement their earnings as performers.

Many musicians belong to a local chapter of the American Federation of Musicians. Professional singers who perform live often belong to a branch of the American Guild of Musical Artists; those who record for the broadcast industries may belong to the American Federation of Television and Radio Artists.

Defining What Dancers Do

Ever since ancient times, dancers have used their bodies to express ideas, stories, rhythm, and sound. In addition to being an art form for its own sake, dance also complements opera, musical comedy, television, movies, music videos, and commercials. Therefore, many dancers sing and act as well as dance.

Dancers most often perform as a group, although a few top artists dance solo. Many dancers combine stage work with teaching or choreographing.

The Range of Opportunities for Dancers

There are four main categories for professional dancers. Following is a brief description of each.

Ballet Dancer

Ballet dancing requires a lot of training—in fact, more than any other kind of dancing. Ballet dancers are performers who express a theme or story.

Modern Dancer

Modern dancers use bodily movements and facial expressions to express ideas and moods. Jazz, though a separate style of dance, is also a more modern approach to dance.

Tap Dancer

Tap dancers use tap shoes to keep time with all kinds of music. The shoes allow them to tap out various dance rhythms.

Choreographer

Choreographers create original dances. They may also create new interpretations of traditional dances, such as the *Nutcracker* ballet, since few dances are written down. Choreographers instruct performers at rehearsals to achieve the desired effect. They also audition performers.

The Life of a Dancer

Dancing is strenuous. Rehearsals require very long hours and usually take place daily, including weekends and holidays. For shows on the road, weekend travel is often necessary. Rehearsals are generally scheduled during the day. Since most performances take place in the evening, dancers usually work late hours.

Due to the physical demands, most dancers stop performing by their late thirties, but they sometimes continue to work in the dance field as choreographers, dance teachers and coaches, or artistic directors. Some celebrated dancers, however, continue performing beyond the age of fifty.

Dancers work in a variety of settings, including dining establishments, theatrical and television productions, dance studios and schools, dance companies and bands, and amusement parks.

In addition, there are many dance instructors in secondary schools, colleges and universities, and private studios. Many teachers also perform from time to time.

New York City is the home of many of the major dance companies. Other cities with full-time professional dance companies include Atlanta, Boston, Chicago, Cincinnati, Cleveland, Columbus, Dallas, Houston, Miami, Milwaukee, Montreal, Philadelphia, Pittsburgh, Salt Lake City, San Francisco, Seattle, Toronto, Vancouver, and Washington, D.C.

Qualifications and Training for Dancers

Training varies with the type of dance and is a continuous part of all dancers' careers. Many dancers and dance instructors believe that dancers should start with a good foundation in classical dance before selecting a particular dance style. Ballet training for women usually begins at five to eight years of age with a private teacher or through an independent ballet school. Serious training traditionally begins between the ages of ten and twelve. Men often begin their ballet training between the ages of ten and fifteen.

Students who demonstrate potential in their early teens receive more intensive and advanced professional training. At about this time, students should begin to focus their training on a particular style and decide whether to pursue additional training through a dance company's school or a college dance program. Leading dance school companies often have summer training programs from which they select candidates for admission to their regular full-time training programs. Formal training for modern and culturally specific dancers often begins later than training in ballet; however, many folk dance forms are taught to very young children.

Many dancers have their first professional auditions by age seventeen or eighteen. Training is an important component of professional dancers' careers. Dancers normally spend eight hours a day in class and rehearsal, keeping their bodies in shape and preparing for performances. Their daily training period includes time to warm up and cool down before and after classes and rehearsals.

Because of the strenuous and time-consuming training required, some dancers view formal education as secondary. However, a broad, general education including music, literature, history, and the visual arts is helpful in the interpretation of dramatic episodes, ideas, and feelings. Dancers sometimes conduct research to learn more about the part they are playing.

Many colleges and universities award bachelor's or master's degrees in dance, typically through departments of music, theater, or fine arts. The National Association of Schools of Dance accredits fifty-seven programs in dance. Many programs concentrate on modern dance, but some also offer courses in jazz, culturally specific, ballet, or classical techniques; dance composition, history, and criticism; and movement analysis.

A college education is not essential to obtaining employment as a professional dancer; however, many dancers obtain degrees in unrelated fields to prepare themselves for careers after dance. The completion of a college program in dance and education is required in order to qualify to teach dance in college, high school, or elementary school. Colleges and conservatories sometimes require graduate degrees but may accept performance experience. A college background is not necessary, however, for teaching dance or choreography in local recreational programs. Studio schools usually require teachers to have experience as performers.

Choreographers typically are older dancers with years of experience in the theater. Through their performance as dancers, they develop reputations that often lead to opportunities to choreograph productions.

Desirable Traits for Dancers

Because of the rigorous practice schedules of most dancers, self-discipline, patience, perseverance, and a devotion to dance are essential for success in the field. Dancers also must possess good problem-solving skills and an ability to work with people. Good health and physical stamina also are necessary attributes. Above all, dancers must have flexibility, agility, coordination, grace, a sense of rhythm, a feeling for music, and a creative ability to express themselves through movement.

Since dancers seldom perform unaccompanied, they must be able to work as part of a team. They should also be highly motivated and prepared to face the anxiety of intermittent employment and rejections when auditioning for work. For dancers, advancement takes the form of a growing reputation, more frequent work, bigger and better roles, and higher pay.

Compensation

The earnings for many professional dancers is governed by union contracts. Dancers in major opera ballet, classical ballet, and modern dance corps belong to the American Guild of Musical Artists, AFL-CIO. Those on live or videotaped television belong to the

American Federation of Television and Radio Artists. Those who perform in films and on television belong to the Screen Actors Guild or the Screen Extras Guild. Those in musical comedies are members of the Actors' Equity Association. The unions and producers sign basic agreements specifying minimum salary rates, hours of work, benefits, and other conditions of employment. However, the contract each dancer signs with the producer of the show may be more favorable than the basic agreement.

Median annual earnings of salaried dancers were $21,100 in 2002. The middle 50 percent earned between $14,570 and $34,660. The lowest 10 percent earned less than $12,880, and the highest 10 percent earned more than $53,350.

Median annual earnings of salaried choreographers were $29,470 in 2002. The middle 50 percent earned between $19,590 and $43,720. The lowest 10 percent earned less than $14,000, and the highest 10 percent earned more than $57,590. Median annual earnings were $29,820 in other schools and instruction, which includes dance studios and schools.

Dancers who were on tour received an additional allowance for room and board, as well as extra compensation for overtime. Earnings from dancing are usually low, because employment is part year and irregular. Dancers often supplement their income by working as guest artists with other dance companies, teaching dance, or taking jobs unrelated to the field.

Dancers covered by union contracts are entitled to some paid sick leave, paid vacations, and various health and pension benefits, including extended sick pay and childbirth provisions. Employers contribute toward these benefits. Most other dancers do not receive any benefits.

Words from the Pros

Several professionals from the worlds of music and dance have shared their stories. Read their accounts to see what a performing career is really like.

Mark Marek, Singer and Dance Band Leader

Mark Marek is a singer and the leader of Private Stock Variety Dance Band of Lenexa, Kansas. His background includes two years of college with course work focusing on music theory, audio engineering, and the fundamentals of music and business.

Mark started playing drums in junior high school and later learned to play the six-string guitar. By age sixteen, he joined his brother's band, and nearly twenty years ago he started a band of his own. Mark describes Private Stock as "a country club, high dollar–type band." They play mostly at weddings, country clubs, and other formal occasions.

The band's working hours are usually 6:30 P.M. until 1 A.M., mostly on Fridays and Saturdays. Most jobs last three to four hours, but the band members must arrive at least an hour and a half before the start time to set up their instruments. They generally perform one-hour sets, with a twenty-minute break every hour or so. After the job, they have to stay to break down the equipment. Since the members have performed together for so many years, they don't need to rehearse more frequently than once every three or four months.

"I love seeing the reaction of the audience," Mark says. "It's fun to know and see that they are having a good time. That's the thrill I get out of it. What I least like is the inconsistency in bookings. Each month the number of gigs changes, which affects the cash flow. The peak periods for the band are December, May, and June."

There is also a business side to managing a band, and Mark spends weekdays taking bookings, arranging schedules, and making telephone calls. He also handles the contracts for each performance. In addition to his work with Private Stock, Mark gives private guitar lessons and books jobs for other bands.

Mark Marek offers some advice to anyone interested in a career similar to his. "To approach success in the music industry, you need to have good people skills, a general sense of business, a real enjoyment for what you do, a recognition of what your niche is in the music world, patience, good customer-relations skills, expert technical skills, and a knowledge of audio and video technology.

"Having a band is a business, not an ego trip. You really need to have a basic knowledge of business and marketing," he stresses. "You can be the best musician, but you have to know how to sell yourself in order to be successful. It's a tough way to make a living—that's why you have to really have a passion for the business."

Priscilla Gale, Singer and Voice Teacher

Soprano Priscilla Gale attended both the Juilliard School of Music and the Cleveland Institute of Music. She has also studied in Austria and with private teachers Luigi Ricci (in Rome) and Michael Trimble. When she's not performing with an opera company or symphony orchestra, Priscilla teaches voice at Wesleyan University in Middletown, Connecticut.

Priscilla comes from a family of musicians, including pianists, singers, and violinists. She began playing piano at age five. Despite assumptions that she would pursue a career as a pianist, Priscilla found her real enjoyment was singing. Once she discovered opera, she knew that she had found her calling. Her first professional singing contract was with the Fort Wayne Symphony Orchestra during her senior year at the Cleveland Institute of Music.

Priscilla tries to explain the somewhat ethereal quality of singing: "Every engagement a singer or performer experiences changes you in the most wonderful way. You, as an artist, grow on multiple levels, both personally and artistically. Each time, your artistic life is changed; you grow in some immeasurable, wonderful way, and the possibilities are limitless."

Working conditions differ at various engagements. Priscilla describes opera rehearsals as intense, usually including ten- to twelve-hour days for two or three weeks. Performances with orchestras generally last over a three- or four-day period. The singer usually has a piano rehearsal with the conductor, then one or two orchestra rehearsals, followed by the performances.

Professional singers must be able to adapt to different working conditions. As Priscilla says, "It is always busy and intense but exciting. It is fast paced, and one must know one's craft. There is little room for poor preparation. And you must always have the ability to adjust to every circumstance and environment, for no two are ever the same. Every conductor is different, every director, and so forth. You must be very adaptable and professional."

Like many dedicated performers, Priscilla gains an intensely personal satisfaction from her work while remaining aware of the realities of the profession.

"What I love most about my work is the ability to touch an audience—people I never meet individually, but collectively," she says. "My heart and soul meet theirs. But there are just not enough performance opportunities for everyone, and it is no longer possible to make a full-time living at this career unless you are one of the lucky top 20 percent."

Priscilla's experience allows her to offer some sound advice to aspiring singers. She says, "I always tell people who want to do this kind of work to look inward and ask if there is anything else in life that will bring them happiness and fulfillment. If so, then I suggest that they do that instead. If not, then they should by all means pursue this career. But know that it is—especially in the beginning—a very complicated business that represents a difficult life.

"Talent is but a small piece of it. Most people cannot comprehend the level of sacrifice that this career requires. There is that wonderful, romantic notion of being the 'starving artist,' but there's nothing romantic about it when you're living it.

"However, with hard work, determination, perseverance, and an unwavering faith in yourself, anything can happen. The journey is an incredible ride, and one I would not have missed. And as I look back at my past, at my present, and toward my future, I can honestly say that I am one of the lucky ones."

Karen Tyler, Singer, Songwriter, and Guitarist

Karen Tyler of Austin, Texas, earned an associate of arts degree from Pepperdine University in Malibu, California. She has been working as a blues singer, songwriter, and guitarist since 1979. Karen has released three CDs, *Lovin' the Blues Too Long* (1997), *Alone & Blue* (2000), and *All Shades of Blue* (2003). The Karen Tyler Band won first-place honors in the 2003 Monterey Bay Blues Festival's Battle of the Bands, after competing with 150 other bands.

"I had a natural talent for singing and found songwriting to be an incredible emotional outlet," says Karen. "And I have developed some pretty good business skills in order to stay in the music business. From the beginning, being front and center stage and being appreciated for my feelings was important to me."

Karen explains that while many artists have to work at other jobs to support their music, she was fortunate not to have to pursue other work. Early in her career she and her husband moved to Texas so that they could afford to live on one salary while Karen worked on her music.

In 1998 they returned to California, where Karen formed her band. She writes the songs for the band and plays both lead and rhythm guitar; she also provides vocals.

Between performing and managing the band, Karen maintains a very full schedule. She keeps a mailing list, creates her own promotional materials, and writes a quarterly newsletter. She handles bookkeeping and accounting of band income and CD and tape sales. Karen also makes demo tapes and mails out promotional packages. To do the best job possible, she does a great deal of research on radio stations, booking agents, clubs, festivals, record companies, and any other aspects of the industry that will promote her music.

"I spend anywhere from one to four hours a day doing just the business of music," Karen says. "In addition, I play several nights a week from two to four hours, sometimes traveling three and four hours to play. Nothing at all may happen for a period of time, and just when I get into a routine I really like, someone will call or an opportunity will arise that will take all of my attention."

Karen acknowledges that the business side of her career often takes precedence over performing. "There is never a time when something like songwriting or practicing guitar doesn't take a back seat to some kind of business duty," she says. "I have tried to get a manager but have had some really bad experiences, and at this point in my career I feel that it is better if I retain the control, even if the responsibilities are a bit overwhelming. Everyone always has a suggestion about what you should be doing to help your career. And you can't possibly do everything people suggest, so making an action plan and sticking to it is the best thing. Trying to be organized is my biggest challenge, and getting things down on paper helps.

"I spend anywhere from twenty-five to thirty hours a week doing music business and play anywhere from four to twelve hours a week. I work from a home office and so it gets a little lonely. My husband is moving his office into the home, which I assume will make it a bit better for me. At least I will have someone to bounce some ideas off. Sometimes I really feel like I'm out there all alone."

Karen talks about the ups and downs of her career: "I enjoy a good crowd response to my music. It makes it all worthwhile when someone comes up and tells me I have an 'amazing voice' or that I play the guitar well or that a certain song really touched them. The worst part is probably that people don't go out as much as they used to. They are 'programmed' by television, radio, and print media as to what to buy and what to listen to or go to see. They get comfortable going to hear certain acts, and until they have heard rave reviews about someone forty or fifty times, they don't make the effort to go and see them. Even when they do, they are liable to slip back into the habit of going where they always go. A side effect is that talent doesn't count as much as who you know and how much fun you are to 'hang out with.'

"On top of that, bands who want to 'make it' are expected to finance their own recordings, put out expensive CDs, and sell literally thousands of them before a record company will consider signing them. This is kind of hard when you are playing for fewer and fewer people every day."

Karen's advice for aspiring singers and songwriters addresses the practical side of the business: "I would advise those interested in this career to go to college and develop a talent (preferably nonmusical) whereby you can create your own business—computers, catering, consulting," she says. "You have to have some way of supporting yourself and coming up with $5,000 to $10,000 every year or two for a CD, and you have to have a flexible schedule so that you can tour and support the CD and work whenever you can."

Kathryn Maffei, Pianist and Music Director

Kathryn Maffei has been playing the piano for more than forty years. She has ten years of classical training with a concert pianist. Kathryn is currently music director at Our Lady of Miracles Church and School in Gustine, California.

"When I started taking piano lessons at eight years old," says Kathryn, "I began to entertain my family. Then I performed for family and friends' parties as well as local club and organization events. Quickly it spread to playing the piano for chorus classes in grammar school and high school bands and entertaining for many different kinds of local events, such as proms, fashion or variety shows, plays, and other social functions."

After she got married, Kathryn took a few years off to raise her family. When her children began to attend school, she went with them to teach music classes, since none of the teachers at their school had musical abilities. Kathryn became the church organist and played at weddings, funerals, and masses.

As her music became known throughout the community, Kathryn began performing at parties in hotels and country clubs, as well as at parties celebrating holidays, birthdays, anniversaries, and class reunions, among other events. She became music director for a local performing arts company and has been piano conductor for over a dozen musical plays, including *Oliver*; *Annie*; *Big River*; *Hello Dolly*; *Bye Bye Birdie*; *Peter Pan*; *You're a Good Man, Charlie Brown*; and *Beauty and the Beast*. Kathryn has also performed for many fund-raising benefits and has served as a judge for local music talent showcases. In addition to her work as music director, Kathryn teaches private piano students and serves as the church's pianist and organist.

Kathryn began working at Our Lady of Miracles thirteen years ago, when the assistant superintendent of schools saw her perform and hired her immediately to teach music at her school. She currently teaches on Mondays and Wednesdays, working from 7:30 A.M. to 3 P.M., and has also served on a visual and performing arts committee to integrate performing arts into the diocesan schools.

"When designing music programs for children, my main concern is to teach a love for the art of music," Kathryn says. "I believe this is best accomplished at the earliest age possible. Hopefully, this is a feeling that will stay with the children all their lives, as it did in mine. It is well known that bringing music and liberal arts to students is important on so many levels and ensures a broad and rich education. The arts reinforce social skills, instill positive attitudes and values, and support growth and intellectual enrichment. The arts serve not only to develop personal intellectual growth, but also sharpen judgment and interpersonal decision making. The key is to start with young children, and I know almost no other way to get and keep a small child's attention than with music.

"I truly love children and music and have never regretted my profession because I get so much enjoyment out of it. It is my life's work as much it would be for an accountant who works with numbers and a lawyer who deals with laws! To others I say, 'Go for it if you feel it is in your heart!'"

Mike Watson, Recording Artist

Mike Watson, head of Watson Entertainment, is a Georgia-based recording artist. He majored in music at West Georgia College and performs regularly with his group, the Mike Watson Band, which has released the CD *Biscuit on My Mind*. He is also a successful producer and will soon open a music production facility for songwriters and artists in Nashville, Tennessee.

"I started playing professionally in 1980 as lead guitarist and harmony singer for a band on the circuit," explains Mike. "I have been fascinated with music as long as I can remember, and I turned that dream into reality with a lot of hard work and perseverance and never settling for second best or taking no for an answer."

A typical day for Mike usually means rising at noon and spending some time doing chores and running errands. He performs from 9 P.M. until 1 or 2 A.M. "Entertaining is what I do," Mike says. "Naturally, it is always a party atmosphere. When I go to different states doing shows, it's somewhat similar except I get to see places and people in one day I probably will never meet and maybe never see again."

"I love almost every part of my job and consider myself to be so very fortunate because I am able to do the one thing I love doing most—making a living at making music.

"My least favorite part is dealing with people who had a little too much to drink and every now and then having to deal with less-than-desirable booking agents who send you to a job that isn't quite what they paint it to be.

Like many artists, Mike believes that success can come from following your dreams. "My advice to others is, if you have a genuine dream, never give up!" Mike says. "If you know in your heart that you have what it takes to succeed in your chosen profession, go for it!"

Chris Murphy, Musician, Record Producer, and DJ

Chris Murphy is a professional musician, entertainer, record producer, and entertainment buyer, as well as a part-time disc jockey. He began music lessons as a teenager, and later he attended Berklee College of Music in Boston. His father was also a musician, and Chris often played in bands with him before going on the road with his own band in 1978.

Chris has released five solo CDs, including *I'm a Happy Guy, On a Blue Afternoon*, and *Broken Wheel*, and has also performed on over a dozen CDs with other artists. He also manages Speakeasy CDs, an independent recording label for blues artists, and cohosts a radio show in Ontario called "Blues Never Die."

"I don't know how to do anything else," says Chris. "Music is one of the few things I was good at and could take pride in. As a teenager, I felt that music stood out as something that was fun and that I excelled at.

"I started playing the saxophone at age seventeen and started playing in bands about the same time. I was in love with the blues long before I became a blues musician."

Chris loves the atmosphere of performing in blues clubs four to six nights a week. He also spends time each day on the telephone, organizing appearances and musicians' schedules. Overall, however, his feelings about his career are positive. As Chris says, "I meet a lot of interesting, talented, and funny people. I receive a lot of respect and love from the audiences I perform for. There is nothing that can replace the feeling of being onstage with a great band on a good night! I also have time to spend with my daughter in the daytime during the week, though occasionally I am away for the weekend.

"I enjoy the fact that when I go out to earn money, I am going out to play. How many people can say that? My advice to others is to never, ever quit. The people who hang in there are the ones who inherit the entertainment business!"

Lionel Ward, Musician

Lionel Ward first became interested in being a musician when he was only nine years old and his mother bought him an Airline guitar for Christmas. Now he tours North America and Europe as the lead singer for the New World Band, an Elvis-tribute group.

Lionel was discovered by the late Wolfman Jack, who noticed his resemblance to Elvis Presley and invited him to a meeting. Lionel's manager then sent a demo tape to Wolfman Jack's record label, Sonic Records, and the New World Band began recording under that label. Lionel and the New World Band have released three CDs, *This One's for You*, *Rockabilly Rebel*, and *All the Girls*.

"I came from a musical family, so there was always music in the house," Lionel says. "Music is therapy for the soul. It is the greatest feeling in the world to be able to play in front of an audience and see the enjoyment you give people. If you can relieve them of the everyday burdens of life for just a few minutes, you've done something important. The natural high you get from doing a live show cannot be compared to anything else. The only way you can achieve this feeling is through the music. And the beautiful thing is that it is all natural. Being able to sing and play an instrument is a God-given talent; you cannot buy this anywhere. You have to be born with it. It is a blessing to be able to share it with your audience."

Lionel stresses how important it is for a performer to give his or her all to every audience. "One thing I learned very early in the entertainment business is that every performance has to be the best you can possibly do," he says. "The key is to be able to sing your songs as if they are being performed for the very first time. It may actually be the thousandth time you have sung that song, but in my opinion, it should be a thousand times better than the first. The people in the audience have chosen to take the time out of their evening to come and hear you play. You do not want to disappoint them, and I always make sure I do my very best, whether there are five people in the audience or five thousand."

In addition to performing, Lionel's role as lead singer means that he is responsible for seeing that all necessary arrangements are made for the band. He determines which lighting and public address systems will be used and how large a road crew will be needed. Such details are important for a successful performance. As Lionel says, "I must ensure that all of this is taken care of because it affects my show tremendously if I cannot hear the band or we can't see because someone forgot to put up a spotlight."

Lionel acknowledges that it is difficult to describe a typical workday in his career. "As far as what work I actually do," he says, "I am involved with every aspect, right down to the last microphone sound check. You cannot measure how many hours are involved because some shows take days. If you count the actual rehearsal time, driving to the gigs, set-up and tear-down times, and sound checks, you would think we were insane. Our lives are devoted to music, but it is a labor of love. Sometimes we are gone from our homes for weeks. Living in hotels, doing radio and television interviews, is not one big party. I am very fortunate because for as long as I have been doing this, I have never considered it work. I truly love what I am doing."

Lionel is fortunate to truly love his work. As he says, "I particularly enjoy recording in the studio because it's like taking a piece of your life and freezing it in time. But I also love performing live. Again, there is no better feeling in the world than when the audience is wrapped up in your song and you are taking them on a journey.

"As far as I can see, there is no downside in this business. I am very fortunate that my wife travels with me and shares my dreams. For some people, I think a downside would be having to leave their family."

Lionel offers encouraging advice to aspiring performers. "My advice to others is to follow your dreams and what you feel in your heart. This business is very rough and unforgiving at times. But if you believe in yourself and you have the burning desire to make it, then you will. This business cannot be measured by hours or even days. It cannot be measured by money, either, though we need money to survive. If you truly believe in yourself and your music, everything else will fall into place.

"Many times you will hear me thank the audience for their support through the years. I was born a poor boy—rich with love and dreams, though—and I am definitely living my dreams!"

John A. Roberts, DJ and Business Owner

John Roberts attended Montgomery College in Rockville, Maryland, majoring in speech and drama; he then attended the University of Maryland at College Park, where he majored in radio and television.

In August of 1996, he competed in the National DJ of the Year competition in Atlantic City and ranked in the top ten DJs nationally. The same year he was awarded the Best Club DJ in Las Vegas by the American DJ Awards. He has spoken at numerous DJ conventions in the United States and Canada and has written articles for magazines such as *Mobile Beat, DJ Times,* and the *ADJA News.*

"I started as a stand-up comic in the late sixties to mid-seventies," says John. "As I was one of the first in this profession, I learned from the 'school of hard knocks.' While in the air force I competed in the air force talent show, the Tops in Blue competition. I won first place in comedy and went on to worldwide competition."

John has owned his own DJ and karaoke business and served as National Operations Manager of the American Disc Jockey Association, which he founded. He also owned the DJ Training Center, the first full-service, independent training facility for disc jockeys in the country.

John first worked as a DJ at the USO club in Washington, D.C., while he was in the air force and decided to make this work a career when he left service in 1975. "I had this totally unique idea," he says. "By acting as DJ and playing records, I would serve as a band for clubs, weddings, and other parties. I could go anywhere and be mobile! I had absolutely no idea that someone else might have this idea, too. I certainly had never heard of it and knew of no one who did it. Many people close to me thought I was crazy and should pursue a real job. No one knew disco was brewing right around the corner. That's when DJs truly became accepted as a form of entertainment.

"I always wanted to get into broadcasting and wanted to keep up with my comedy. But after doing stand-up comedy and doing stage shows in high school and college, I loved the live audience. I figured that being a mobile DJ could be a stepping-stone in both directions."

John enjoyed working for a live crowd as opposed to working in radio. The spontaneous reactions of the crowd and the ability to be self-employed at a job he loved added to his determination to make his career a success.

As with any business, there is also a practical side that must be addressed. John deals with legal contracts, promotion, marketing, advertising, bookkeeping, and staffing issues. He must also order and maintain his inventory of music and equipment.

John's usual work schedule is quite full. He answers phone calls and responds to customers' inquiries; handles contract negotiations; trains DJs; prepares schedules; makes advertising decisions; and creates and prints karaoke catalogs. At night he performs at a party. This part of the job requires acting as coordinator between the host and the guests, handling guests' requests, and trying to keep everyone entertained.

"What I like most about this career is that I am my own boss," John says. "I can pick and choose the shows I do. I get to work in exciting places and meet exciting, sometimes famous people. Being a mobile DJ has lead to some interesting job opportunities for me. I did a television show like "American Bandstand" for more than three years. I was a part of thirty to forty radio and television commercials, performed on radio, served as one of the original hosts of the Home Shopper's Club of Virginia, auditioned for a movie, and have been able to travel all over the United States.

"On the downside, there are no benefits that you ordinarily receive from an employer (unless you are willing to pay for them). It's very hard on my personal social life. My average time to get to sleep is three or four in the morning."

John suggests that anyone interested in a career as a mobile DJ should consider all aspects of the career. "My advice is that people should realize this is a business and it must be treated as such. I'd advise others never to burn bridges. Create friendly competitors and network, network, network. Learn to entertain—to think on your feet. Always be willing to learn new tricks and techniques to stay on top. The minute you think you know it all is the minute your competition starts getting ahead of you."

For More Information

There are literally hundreds of professional associations for musicians and dancers. Contact any of the following for more information about employment in these fields.

Musicians

American Choral Directors Association (ACDA)
54 Couch Drive
Oklahoma City, OK 73102
www.acdaonline.org

American Federation of Musicians (AFM)
New York Headquarters
1501 Broadway, Suite 600
New York, NY 10036
or

Canadian Office
75 The Donway West, Suite 1010
Don Mills, ON M3C 2E9
Canada
www.afm.org

American Federation of Television and Radio Artists (AFTRA)
New York National Office
260 Madison Avenue
New York, NY 10016
or
Los Angeles National Office
5757 Wilshire Boulevard, Ninth Floor
Los Angeles, CA 90036
www.aftra.org

American Guild of Musical Artists (AGMA)
1430 Broadway, Fourteenth Floor
New York, NY 10018
www.musicalartists.org

American Guild of Organists (AGO)
475 Riverside Drive, Suite 1260
New York, NY 10115
www.agohq.org

American Guild of Music (AGM)
PO Box 599
Warren, MI 48090
www.americanguild.org

American Music Conference (AMC)
5790 Armada Drive
Carlsbad, CA 92008
www.amc-music.com

American Musicological Society
201 South Thirty-Fourth Street
University of Pennsylvania
Philadelphia, PA 19104
www.ams-net.org

American Symphony Orchestra League (ASOL)
910 Seventeenth Street NW
Washington, DC 20006
www.symphony.org

Academy of Country Music (ACM)
4100 West Alameda Avenue, Suite 208
Burbank, CA 91505
www.acmcountry.com

Broadcast Education Association
National Association of Broadcasters
1771 N Street NW
Washington, DC 20036
www.beaweb.org

Broadcast Music, Inc. (BMI)
320 West Fifty-Seventh Street
New York, NY 10019
www.bmi.com

Chamber Music America
305 Seventh Avenue, Fifth Floor
New York, NY 10001
www.chamber-music.org

Chorus America
1156 Fifteenth Street NW, Suite 310
Washington, DC 20005
www.chorusamerica.org

College Music Society
312 East Pine Street
Missoula, MT 59802
www.music.org

Concert Artists Guild (CAG)
850 Seventh Avenue, Suite 1205
New York, NY 10019
www.concertartists.org

Country Music Association (CMA)
One Music Circle South
Nashville, TN 37203
www.cmaworld.com

Gospel Music Association (GMA)
1205 Division Street
Nashville, TN 37203
www.gospelmusic.org

International Alliance for Women in Music (IAWM)
Box 2731
Rollins College
1000 Holt Avenue
Winter Park, FL 32789
www.iawm.org

International Conference of Symphony and Opera Musicians
    (ICSOM)
www.icsom.org

Metropolitan Opera Association (MOA)
Lincoln Center
New York, NY 10023
www.metopera.org

National Academy of Popular Music
Songwriters Hall of Fame
330 West Fifty-Eighth Street, Suite 411
New York, NY 10017
www.songwritershalloffame.org

National Academy of Recording Arts and Sciences (NARAS)
The Recording Academy
3402 Pico Boulevard
Santa Monica, CA 90405
www.grammy.com

National Association of Schools of Music
11250 Roger Bacon Drive, Suite 21
Reston, VA 22091
http://nasm.arts-accredit.org

National Music Council
425 Park Street
Montclair, NJ 07043
www.musiccouncil.org

National Symphony Orchestra Association (NSOA)
National Conducting Institute
John F. Kennedy Center for the Performing Arts
2700 F Street NW
Washington, DC 20566
www.kennedy-center.org/nso/conducting.html

Opera America
1156 Fifteenth Street NW, Suite 810
Washington, DC 20005
www.operaamerica.org

Orchestra Canada
56 The Esplanade, Suite 203
Toronto, ON M5E 1A7
Canada
www.oc.ca

Radio-Television News Directors Association/Foundation
   (RTNDA/RTNDF)
1600 K Street NW, Suite 700
Washington, DC 20006
www.rtndf.org

Screen Actors Guild (SAG)
Los Angeles Office
5757 Wilshire Boulevard
Hollywood, CA 90036
www.sag.org

Society of Professional Audio Recording Services
9 Music Square South, Suite 222
Nashville, TN 37203
www.spars.com

Dancers

For information on directories of colleges and universities that
teach dance, including details on the types of courses offered and
available scholarships, write to:

National Dance Association
American Alliance for Health, Physical Education, Recreation
   and Dance (AAHPERD)
1900 Association Drive
Reston, VA 20190
www.aahperd.org/nda

A directory of dance programs, as well as art and design, music, and theater programs, may be obtained from:

National Association of Schools of Dance
11250 Roger Bacon Drive, Suite 21
Reston, VA 20190
http://nasd.arts-accredit.org

For information on all aspects of dance, including job listings, send a self-addressed stamped envelope to:

American Dance Guild
PO Box 2006
Lenox Hill Station
New York, NY 10021
www.americandanceguild.org

A directory of dance companies and related organizations, plus other information on professional dance, is available from:

Dance/USA
1156 Fifteenth Street NW, Suite 820
Washington, DC 20005
www.danceusa.org

CHAPTER THREE

Careers in Politics

When a man assumes a public trust, he should
consider himself as public property.
—Thomas Jefferson

Are you drawn to important issues that face the country and our world? Do you aspire to serve your fellow men and women in a very special way? Do you enjoy the idea of being in the center of the public eye? Then consider following a path to a political career.

Defining What Political Professionals Do

At the top of the political hierarchy are public office holders, including mayors, governors, supervisors, senators, representatives, and, of course, the president and vice president of the country. All of these individuals are elected to administer government. They handle all of the business of a city, town, state, county, or the country as a whole. They must pass laws to keep order, set up special programs to benefit people, and spend the taxpayers' money on goods and services. As problem solvers, they meet with community leaders to find out the needs of the people, and then they search for ways to meet those needs.

There are many other levels of political careers—all the way down to the local levels. This would include those who work for political change in their neighborhoods and those in an official capacity, such as precinct captain. Some jobs are voluntary, unpaid positions that could eventually lead to paying positions. All positions except appointed government managers are elected by their constituents. Nonelected managers are hired by a local government council or commission.

Chief Executives and Legislators

Government chief executives, like their counterparts in the private sector, have overall responsibility for the operation of their organizations. Working with legislators, they set goals and arrange programs to attain them. They appoint department heads to oversee the civil servants who carry out programs enacted by legislative bodies. Chief executives in government oversee budgets and ensure that resources are used properly and that programs are carried out as planned.

The duties of government chief executives also include meeting with legislators and constituents to determine the level of support for proposed programs. In addition, they often nominate citizens to boards and commissions, encourage business investment, and promote economic development in their communities. To do all of these varied tasks effectively, chief executives of large governments rely on a staff of highly skilled aides to research issues that concern the public. Executives who control small governmental bodies, however, often do this work by themselves.

Legislators are elected officials who develop, enact, or amend laws. They include United States senators and representatives, state senators and representatives, and county, city, and town commissioners and council members.

Legislators introduce, examine, and vote on bills to pass official legislation. In preparing such legislation, they study staff reports and hear testimony from constituents, representatives of interest groups, board and commission members, and others with an interest in the issue under consideration. They usually must approve budgets and the appointments of nominees for leadership posts whose names are submitted by the chief executive. In some bodies, the legislative council appoints the city, town, or county manager.

Both chief executives and legislators perform many ceremonial duties, such as opening new buildings, making proclamations, welcoming visitors, and leading celebrations. It is both a privilege and an important responsibility to serve in public office.

Working Conditions

The working conditions of legislators and government chief executives vary with the size and budget of the governmental unit. Time spent at work ranges from a few hours a week for some local leaders to stressful weeks of sixty or more hours for members of the U.S. Congress. Similarly, some jobs require only occasional out-of-town travel, while others involve long periods away from home, such as when attending sessions of the legislature.

United States senators and representatives, governors and lieutenant governors, and chief executives and legislators in municipalities work full-time, year-round, as do most county and city managers. Many state legislators work full-time on government business while the legislature is in session (usually for two to six months a year or every other year) and work only part-time when the legislature is not in session.

Some local elected officials work a schedule that is officially designated as part-time but actually is the equivalent of a full-time schedule when unpaid duties are taken into account. In addition to their regular schedules, most chief executives are on call to handle emergencies.

Qualifications and Training

Apart from meeting minimum age, residency, and citizenship requirements, candidates for legislative positions have no established training or qualifications criteria. Candidates come from a wide variety of occupations, such as lawyers, private-sector managers or executives, or business owners. In addition, many do have some political experience as staffers or members of government bureaus, boards, or commissions. Successful candidates usually become well-known through their political campaigns, and some have built voter name recognition through their work with community religious, fraternal, or social organizations.

Increasingly, candidates target information to voters through advertising paid for by their respective campaigns, so fund-raising skills are essential to those hoping to win elections. Management-level work experience and public service help to develop the fund-raising, budgeting, public-speaking, and problem-solving skills that are needed to run an effective political campaign.

Candidates must be able to make decisions quickly, sometimes on the basis of limited or contradictory information. They also should be able to inspire and motivate their constituents and staff. Additionally, they must know how to reach compromises and satisfy the often conflicting demands of their constituents. National, state, and even some local campaigns require massive amounts of energy and stamina, traits vital to successful candidates.

Virtually all town, city, and county managers have at least a bachelor's degree, and many hold a higher degree. A master's in public administration is best, including courses in public financial management and legal issues in public administration.

Working in management support positions in government is a prime source of the experience and personal contacts required to eventually secure a manager position. For example, future managers often gain experience as management analysts or assistants in government departments, working for committees, councils, or chief executives. In this capacity, they learn about planning, budgeting, civil engineering, and other aspects of running a government. With sufficient experience, they may be hired to manage a small government.

Town, city, or county managers generally start by working in a smaller community and advancing to larger municipalities as they gain experience. A broad knowledge of local issues, combined with communication skills and the ability to compromise, are essential for advancement in this field.

Advancement opportunities for elected officials are not clearly defined. Because elected positions normally require a period of residency and because local public support is critical, officials usually advance to other offices only in the jurisdictions where they live. For example, council members may run for mayor or for a position in the state government, and state legislators may run for governor or for the U.S. Congress. Many officials are not politically ambitious, however, and do not seek advancement. Others lose their bids for reelection or voluntarily leave the occupation. A lifetime career as a government chief executive or legislator is unusual.

Compensation

Earnings of public administrators vary widely, depending on the size of the government unit and on whether the job is part-time, full-time and year-round, or full-time for only a few months a year. Salaries range from little or nothing for a town council member to $400,000 a year for the president of the United States. The National Conference of State Legislatures reports that the annual salary for rank-and-file legislators in the forty states that paid an annual salary ranged from $10,000 to more than $99,000 in 2003. In eight states, legislators received a daily salary plus an allowance for living expenses while legislatures were in session.

The Council of State Governments reports in its *Book of the States 2002–2003* that gubernatorial annual salaries ranged from $50,000 in American Samoa to $179,000 in New York. In addition to a salary, most governors received benefits such as transportation and an official residence.

In 2003, U.S. senators and representatives earned $154,700, the senate and house majority and minority leaders earned $171,900, and the vice president was paid $198,600.

Median annual earnings of legislators were $15,220 in 2002. The middle 50 percent earned between $13,180 and $38,540. The lowest 10 percent earned less than $12,130, and the highest 10 percent earned more than $69,380.

....

Words from the Pros

Following are the personal accounts of three people who work in different aspects of politics. Perhaps their experiences will spark your interest in this field.

Vera Marie Badertscher, Campaign Manager and Consultant

Vera Marie Badertscher earned both B.A. and B.S. degrees in education from Ohio State University in 1960. She went on to secure an M.F.A. from Arizona State University in 1976, focusing on theater. Early in her career, Vera worked primarily as a campaign manager, but later she switched to campaign consultant. She currently works as a freelance writer.

"I started as a citizen volunteer in city projects," she explains. "As a young mother, I wanted a better library system in Scottsdale, Arizona, where I lived, so I volunteered for a committee. There I met officeholders, was invited to serve on their advisory committees, and eventually asked for and received pay for managing a city council election campaign.

"I enjoyed the sense of accomplishment I got from working in politics—of being able to promote my beliefs and make things happen," Vera says. "I also enjoyed the fact that most people involved in politics are action oriented, optimistic true believers. My chief asset was an ability to figure out the best way to communicate political messages and move people to action."

Vera did volunteer work in a federated woman's club, an experience that taught her a great deal. She gained valuable experience, including "bringing diverse people together to work on projects;

combining government and private energies; communicating; and organizing projects. My theater background helped me focus on short-term, collaborative projects."

As a campaign manager, Vera spent most of her working time communicating with volunteers, either by telephone or in memos and newsletters. The limited time of a political campaign makes the job very intense, and quick decision making becomes a vital part of a campaign manager's duties. She says, "Someone advised me when I managed my first congressional campaign that during the last couple of weeks of the campaign, I would be making a dozen decisions every hour and one in twenty or so would be truly important."

In addition, a successful campaign manager must be able to prioritize. It is important to know the difference between the decisions that do not affect the outcome of an election and those that do.

Vera summarizes the work of a campaign manager: "A campaign manager rounds up all the diverse interest groups, volunteers, the candidate and his or her family, advertising personnel, researchers, and fund-raisers. The key to being successful is keeping the focus on what will get the candidate elected and not allowing anyone in the campaign to draw the focus in another direction. You can expect to talk on the phone all day, check off on other people's work, and stay close to the candidate to keep him or her on track. Generally, you are trying to keep the budget down, so the work surroundings are on the primitive side—borrowed furniture and unpainted walls. You can count on noise and constant activity. (If it's quiet, you're probably losing.) This presents a hard atmosphere to concentrate in, but that's the job."

The work of a campaign consultant, by contrast, is somewhat less hectic. She says, "A campaign consultant has more luxury of time to think than does a campaign manager. The consultant typically analyzes voting data history; studies the candidate, the opponent, and the voters; and writes a strategic plan for bringing the voters to support that candidate. Some consultants specialize in media or mail, but I have been a generalist, doing strategy and writing direct mail. The consultant works in an office or home office and meets weekly or biweekly with the candidate, the campaign manager, and others involved in the campaign. Once the plan is written, the consultant is available to help with fine-tuning, to help make adjustments, to help review media plans, to help determine what to ask in polling, and to help interpret the results. While the campaign manager's job is not done until the polls close on election day, the consultant's job is done a few days prior to the election when no more mail can be sent or advertising launched that will affect the outcome."

Vera is frank about the aspects of her job that she likes and dislikes: "I most like the ability to work out the puzzles involved in bringing together the circumstances, the candidate, and the voters in order to persuade them that they will be better off to elect that candidate. I like the thinking and the communicating of politics.

"What I least like is having to be nice to a bunch of people that I might not particularly like or admire. However, I have been fortunate in being able to choose the candidates I work for, so I have worked for people I believe in and personally support. However, politics is about coalition building, so sometimes the expression 'politics makes strange bedfellows' is all too true."

Vera Marie Badertscher offers a few suggestions for aspiring campaign managers: "I would advise anyone interested in entering this kind of work to introduce yourself to a candidate you admire and volunteer to help. Political science classes teach theory, but only campaigning teaches campaigning. Don't try to tell the candidate how to run his or her campaign or volunteer to be the brains behind the organization until you have actually done some of the grunt work of campaigning and learned it from the inside out. You'd be surprised how many people come to a campaign manager and say, 'I'm really good at strategy,' when all the campaign manager really needs is someone to go out in a pickup truck and put up signs. And before any of that—register to vote. Read up on the issues. And last but not least—vote!"

Wade Hyde, Political Consultant

Wade Hyde earned a B.A. in education and history from East Texas State University in Commerce, Texas. He then received an M.A. in urban affairs from the University of Texas at Arlington and an M.A. in civic affairs teaching from the University of Dallas in Irving, Texas. He has served as a campaign manager volunteer consultant, as a civic volunteer board member, and as a planning and zoning commission member in Irving, Texas. Wade has also served as a member of the regional transportation board and member and officer of the Visiting Nurses Association.

"In 1980, I began volunteering in organizations supporting interests with legislative agendas," Wade says. "Political events were at the center of what I found to be most interesting and exciting in earlier years. These events included listening to the presidential nominating conventions on the radio (before pollsters and analysts took all the fun and suspense out of final outcomes) and waiting in the town square for the results of local elections on hot Saturday nights in June.

"History studies and government were naturally interesting and easy for me. No other subject particularly intrigued me. Politics and policy are my calling."

Wade explains that there are different types of political campaigns. The work is seasonal, although the type of campaign (local, regional, or national) determines whether the season lasts three months or two years. Local campaigns usually last about three months, so the job is very intense with the work concentrated into such a short length of time.

In addition, many candidates in local elections know very little about such issues as fund-raising, coalition building, or voter lists, making the campaign manager's job even more stressful. "The nature of the political candidate is usually one of tremendous energy and strong ego with an unshakable belief that the voting populace cannot live without his or her leadership," he says. "The consultant, on the other hand, must bring some order and a consistent, coherent message to the candidate and the workers. The atmosphere is one of chaotic, pressure-cooker days and nights."

Given the intensity of the work, it is not surprising that Wade would acknowledge some negative aspects of the job. As he says, "Everything is always late, unexpected, and includes last-minute and last-second decision making—sometimes like flipping a coin and forging ahead or backtracking. The days start as if the nights had never quit, and each workday lasts about eighteen hours. Both the candidate and campaign workers contract battle fatigue that doesn't end until weeks after election day. Saturdays and Sundays are not exempt."

Fortunately, there is a bright side to the challenges of being a political consultant. "Each new campaign and candidate comes with the promise of a better day and a better way. It's exciting and hopeful to be involved in making a positive change by helping elect someone who can make a big difference. At least that's the upside. The downside is the exhaustion and condensed pressure of a compact campaign effort and, if such should occur, the loss of the candidate's best effort."

Wade offers his view on how to prepare for campaign work: "I would advise others interested in entering this field to understand fully and honestly why you are working for a candidate. Know if you're primarily in it for a job, an appointment, for the experience and excitement, or for the candidate. Be realistic and don't hang around too long because burnout can set in quite soon. See *Wag the Dog* and *Primary Colors*—I found them to be pretty accurate as campaign compilations."

K. Mark Takai, State Representative

K. Mark Takai earned a bachelor of arts degree in political science in 1990 and a master of public health degree in health education in 1993 from the University of Hawaii at Manoa. During his internship for his master's degree, he worked for a city council member for the city and county of Honolulu.

"My experiences at the University of Hawaii while an undergraduate student, graduate student, and employee probably attracted me to the state capitol," he says. "It was through these years that I had the most interaction with the legislators. I now serve as an elected state representative representing District 34, part of Aiea and part of Pearl City (both located near Pearl Harbor on Oahu)."

Mark first became interested in elected office when he was involved in student government in fourth grade. This involvement continued through high school and college, where he served as student body president representing twenty-four hundred students and twelve thousand students, respectively. He declared his candidacy for public office in July 1994, won the primary election in September, and was declared the winner of the seat after the general election in November.

"The job of a state representative runs the gamut," Mark says. "There are probably three different 'jobs' of an elected official— very diverse, but all very important. The first is my job as a community leader. This is probably the most rewarding part of being in public office. The interaction with the community—through schools, community organizations, neighborhood board meetings, and so on—all provide me with the opportunity to listen and then respond to the desires and concerns of the public.

"This part of the job can also be very difficult. I have been very fortunate in that I have not had too many difficult meetings with the public; however, as a freeway project is currently being planned and the project calls for possible public condemnation of private property, I have had my fair share of angry constituents. Most times, though, I am able to work with the residents of our community to address their concerns.

"The second part of my job is as a lawmaker. Constitutionally, this is my most important responsibility. Seventy-five legislators decide what laws are passed.

"My third responsibility is as a politician (a political candidate). This is a very time-consuming process. The 'campaign season' begins around July of even-numbered years and doesn't end until the general election in early November. Aside from raising money to run a successful campaign (marketing materials, brochures, advertisements, and so on), the most difficult and time-consuming tasks of the political season are sign waving (waving to cars along the roadside in the mornings and afternoons) and door-to-door canvassing." (Since winning his first election in 1994, Mark has run four successful reelection campaigns for two-year terms.)

Mark's typical workday depends on the time of year. During the legislative session, from January to May, he begins his day with a 7:30 A.M. breakfast meeting, followed by committee meetings at the state capitol beginning by 9 A.M. The legislators hold private meetings in their offices and catch up on phone calls and messages prior to the House floor session at noon. He eats lunch with constituents or attends a luncheon meeting after the floor session. Committee hearings begin at 2 P.M. and last until 7 P.M. The day usually ends with community meetings that run until about 10 P.M. Saturdays are generally spent at committee hearings or community events. Takai reserves Friday evenings and Sundays for time with his family.

The months when the legislature is not in session or he is not running a reelection campaign do not necessarily afford slow workdays. As Mark says, "I usually work in the office planning for upcoming events. As the state cochairman of Hawaii's Children and Youth in October and as the state chairman of Hawaii's Junior Miss Scholarship Program, I find myself sometimes even busier than during the legislative session."

It is not surprising that this challenging career has its ups and downs. Mark describes his feelings about the job: "The period of nonsession months during the campaign season is really tough and grueling. And, including time spent at receptions, dinners, and so on, I probably spend about seventy hours a week working.

"However, the people I work with (both in the state capitol and throughout the community) make my job most rewarding. I would not trade the experiences that I have had for any other job. Although it can be very stressful and time consuming, I truly enjoy my job as a state representative.

"I derive great pleasure from doing for others. For instance, one of my most rewarding moments occurred when I was able to provide assistance in getting funds to build a new traffic signal at an intersection that saw many near accidents, numerous accidents, and one fatality.

"The least enjoyable part of my job is knowing full well that every bill that we pass and that becomes law has a negative impact on someone or on a specific profession. Although I have voted for many bills that do much good for our community overall, sometimes it is these same bills that get people laid off from their jobs, and so forth. Knowing this causes me great pain."

Mark has some advice for those interested in running for public office: "I would encourage anyone interested in pursuing this kind of career to talk to people about what their concerns are. Meet with various leaders in your community. Get involved with political campaigns or volunteer or work for an elected official. And if you are truly serious, begin your plans for an eventual run for public office. Good luck!"

For More Information

Information on appointed officials in local government can be obtained from:

International City/County Management Association
777 North Capitol Street NE, Suite 500
Washington, DC 20002
www.icma.org

Here are some additional resources:

Democratic National Committee
Young Democrats of America
430 South Capitol Street SE
Washington, DC 20003
www.democrats.org

Republication National Committee
310 First Street SE
Washington, DC 20003
www.rnc.org

The Congressional Management Foundation
513 Capitol Court NE, Suite 300
Washington, DC 20002
www.cmfweb.org

United States Office of Personnel Management
1900 E Street NW
Washington, DC 20415
www.opm.gov

USAJOBS
www.usajobs.opm.gov
 *USAJOBS is the federal government's official source for federal jobs
 and employment information. Visitors to the website can search
 thousands of federal jobs, create and submit a resume, and download
 forms.*

CHAPTER FOUR

Careers in Retail, Service, and Manufacturing Sales

The capitalist system does not guarantee that everybody will become rich, but it guarantees that anybody can become rich.
—Raul R. deSales

HELP WANTED: We are a provider of medical, scientific, and technology research information to academic, corporate, and government markets. Our company is seeking a western region field sales rep. Responsibilities include maintaining customer databases, generating and qualifying sales leads, negotiating sales agreements, representing the company at trade shows, and preparing weekly sales reports. The position requires 50 percent travel. Our ideal candidate will have a four-year college degree with a minimum of three years of outside sales experience, preferably within the information industry. We are looking for a self-motivated individual who has a working knowledge of the Internet, excellent verbal and written communication skills, and computer literacy.

Does the job described in this want ad appeal to you? If it does, you should know that it represents only one of a broad range of possibilities in this field. Many extroverts find their special niche in the world of sales, helping meet the needs of consumers in as many ways as there are products or services to sell.

Defining What Sales Professionals Do

Sales professionals must know how to interact well with others in order to determine the needs and desires of potential buyers and how these needs can best be met. The better that salespeople know their products, and the more at ease they are with others, the more successful they will be in their sales careers. Sales offers many opportunities in a range of positions, products and services, businesses and industries, and locations.

For this book, general sales is broken into the following primary categories:

- Retail
- Services
- Manufacturing and Wholesale

Industry-specific sales careers in insurance, real estate, and travel are covered in Chapter 5.

Retail Sales

Millions of dollars are spent each and every day on all types of merchandise—everything from shoes and books to food and furniture.

Whether selling clothing, cosmetics, or automobiles, a sales worker's primary job is to interest customers in the merchandise. This may be done by describing the product's features, demonstrating its use, showing various models and colors, and pointing out how the product will benefit the customer or client.

For some jobs, particularly those involving the selling of expensive and complex items, special knowledge or skills are needed.

For example, workers who sell personal computers or home electronics must be able to explain to customers the features of various brands and models, the meaning of manufacturers' specifications, and the types of options that are available.

In other jobs that require selling standardized articles—food, hardware, linens, and housewares, for example—sales workers may often do little more than take payments and bag purchases.

Some retail sales workers also receive cash, check, and charge payments; handle returns; and give change and receipts. Depending on the hours they work, they may have to open or close the cash register. This may include counting the money in the cash register; separating charge slips, coupons, and exchange vouchers; and making deposits at the cash office. Sales workers are often held responsible for the contents of their registers and, in many organizations, repeated shortages are cause for dismissal.

In addition, sales workers may help stock shelves or racks, arrange for mailing or delivery of a purchase, mark price tags, take inventory, and prepare displays. Sales workers must be aware of the promotions their stores are sponsoring, as well as those that are sponsored by competitors. Also, they often must recognize possible security risks and know how to handle such situations.

Consumers often form their impressions of a store by its sales force. The retail industry is very competitive and, increasingly, employers are stressing the importance of providing courteous and efficient service. When a customer wants a product that is not on the sales floor, for example, the sales worker may check the stockroom and, if there are none there, place a special order or call another store to locate the item.

Job Settings

Sales workers are employed by many types of retailers to assist customers in the selection and purchase of merchandise. They work in stores ranging from small specialty shops employing a few workers to giant department stores that employ hundreds of salespeople. The largest employers of retail salespeople are department stores, clothing and accessories stores, building material and garden equipment and supplies dealers, and motor vehicle dealers.

In addition, some sales workers are self-employed representatives of direct-sales companies and mail-order houses. Catalog and online sales are two more areas that provide avenues for those interested in venturing into retail sales as a career.

This occupation offers many opportunities for part-time work and is especially appealing to students, retirees, and others seeking to supplement their incomes. However, most of those selling "big-ticket" items, such as cars, jewelry, furniture, and electronic equipment, work full-time and have substantial experience.

Qualifications and Training

There usually are no formal education requirements for this type of work, although a high school diploma or equivalent is preferred. Employers look for people who enjoy working with others and who have the tact and patience to deal with difficult customers. Other desirable characteristics are an interest in sales work, a neat appearance, and the ability to communicate clearly and effectively. The ability to speak more than one language may be helpful for employment in multi-ethnic communities.

Before hiring a salesperson, some employers may conduct a background check, especially for a job selling high-priced items. After hiring, some retailers subject employees to random drug screening tests.

In most small stores, an experienced employee or the proprietor instructs newly hired sales personnel in making out sales checks and operating cash registers. In large stores, training programs are more formal and are usually conducted over several days. Topics generally discussed are customer service, security, the store's policies and procedures, and how to work a cash register.

Depending on the type of product they are selling, employees may be given additional specialized training by manufacturers' representatives. For example, those working in cosmetics receive instruction on the types of products the store carries and how to determine which customers would most benefit from each product. Likewise, employees who sell cars may be required to participate in training programs designed to provide information on the technical details of standard and optional equipment available on new models. Many employers provide periodic training to keep their workers' skills and knowledge current.

As salespeople gain experience and seniority, they usually move to positions of greater responsibility and may be given their choice of departments in which to work. This often means moving to areas with potentially higher earnings and commissions. The highest earnings potential usually is found in selling big-ticket items, although such a position often requires the most knowledge of the product and the greatest talent for persuasion.

Opportunities for advancement vary. In some small stores, advancement is limited because one person, often the owner, does most of the managerial work. In others, some salespeople are promoted to assistant managers. Traditionally, capable salespeople without college degrees could advance to management positions. Today, however, large retail businesses usually prefer to hire college graduates as management trainees, making a college education increasingly important. Despite this trend, motivated and capable employees without college degrees still may advance to administrative or supervisory positions in large establishments.

Retail selling experience may be an asset when one is applying for sales positions with larger retailers or in other industries, such as financial services, wholesale trade, or manufacturing.

Compensation

The starting wage for many retail sales positions is the federal minimum wage, which was $5.15 an hour in 2005. In areas where employers have difficulty attracting and retaining workers, wages tend to be higher than the legislated minimum.

Median hourly earnings of retail salespeople, including commission, were $8.51 in 2002. The middle 50 percent earned between $7.08 and $11.30 an hour. The lowest 10 percent earned less than $6.18; the highest 10 percent earned more than $16.96 an hour. Median hourly earnings in the industries employing the largest numbers of retail salespersons in 2002 were as follows:

Automobile dealers	$18.25
Building material and supplies dealers	$10.41
Department stores	$8.12
Other general merchandise stores	$7.84
Clothing stores	$7.77

Compensation systems vary by type of establishment and merchandise sold. Salespeople receive hourly wages, commissions, or a combination of wages and commissions. Under a commission system, salespeople receive a percentage of the sales that they make. This system offers sales workers the opportunity to increase their earnings considerably, but they may find that their earnings strongly depend on their ability to sell the product and on the ups and downs of the economy. Employers may use incentive programs such as awards, banquets, bonuses, and profit-sharing plans to promote teamwork among the sales staff.

Benefits may be limited in smaller stores, but benefits in large establishments usually are comparable to those offered by other employers. In addition, nearly all salespeople are able to buy their store's merchandise at a discount, with the savings depending upon the type of merchandise.

Service Sales

Service sales representatives are involved in selling a wide variety of services. For example, sales representatives for data processing firms sell complex services such as inventory control, payroll processing, sales analysis, and financial reporting systems. Hotel sales representatives contact government, business, and social groups to solicit convention and conference business for the hotel. Sales representatives for temporary help services firms locate and acquire clients who will hire the firms' employees.

Telephone service sales representatives visit commercial customers to review their telephone systems, analyze their communications needs, and recommend services such as installation of additional equipment. Other representatives sell automotive leasing, public utility, burial, shipping, protective, and management consulting services.

Service sales representatives act as industry experts, consultants, and problem solvers when selling their firm's services. In some cases, the sales representative creates demand for his or her firm's services. A prospective client might be asked to consider buying a particular service it may never have used before; in fact, clients are sometimes not even aware of the need for certain services. For example, wholesalers might be persuaded to order a list of credit ratings for checking their customers' credit records prior to making sales and discover that the list could be used to solicit new business.

There are several different categories of service sales jobs. Outside sales representatives call on clients and prospects at their homes or offices. They may make appointments, or they may practice "cold calls," arriving without any prior notice. Inside sales representatives work on their employers' premises, assisting clients interested in the firms' services. Telemarketing sales representatives sell exclusively over the telephone. They make large numbers of calls to prospects, attempting to sell the service themselves or to arrange an appointment between the prospect and an outside sales representative. Some sales representatives deal exclusively with one, or a few, major clients.

Despite the diversity of services being sold, the jobs of all service sales representatives are very similar. All sales representatives must fully understand and be able to discuss the services their companies offer.

Also, the procedures they follow are similar. Many sales representatives develop lists of prospective clients through telephone and business directories, asking business associates and customers for leads, and calling on new businesses as they cover their assigned territory. Some service sales representatives acquire clients through client inquiries about the company's services.

Regardless of how they first meet the client, all service sales representatives must explain how the services being offered can meet the clients' needs. This often involves demonstrations of the company's services. Sales reps must answer questions about the nature and cost of the services and try to overcome objections in order to persuade potential customers to purchase services. If they fail to make a sale on the first visit, they may follow up with more visits, letters, or phone calls. After closing a sale, service sales representatives generally follow up to see that the purchase meets the customer's needs and to determine if additional services can be sold.

Because service sales representatives obtain many of their new accounts through referrals, their success hinges on developing a satisfied clientele who will continue to use the services and will recommend them to other potential customers. As in other types of sales jobs, a good reputation is crucial to success.

Service sales work varies with the kind of service sold. Selling highly technical services, such as communications systems or computer consulting services, involves complex and lengthy sales negotiations. In addition, sales of such complex services may require extensive after-sale support. In these situations, sales representatives may operate as part of a team of sales representatives and experts from other departments. Sales representatives receive valuable technical assistance from these experts. For example, those who sell data processing services might work with a systems engineer or computer scientist, and those who sell telephone services might receive technical assistance from a communications consultant. Teams enhance customer service and build strong, long-term relationships with customers, resulting in increased sales.

Because of the length of time between the initial contact with a customer and the actual sale, representatives who sell complex technical services generally work with several customers simultaneously. Sales representatives must be well organized and efficient in scheduling their time.

Selling less complex services, such as linen supply or exterminating services, generally involves simpler and shorter sales negotiations.

A sales representative's job may likewise vary with the size of the employer. Those working for large companies generally are more specialized and are assigned territorial boundaries, a specific line of services, and their own accounts. In smaller companies, sales representatives may have broader responsibilities: administrative, marketing, or public relations, for example, in addition to their sales duties.

Job Settings

Service sales representatives hold more than half a million jobs nationwide. More than half of these jobs are in firms providing business services, including computer and data processing, advertising, personnel supply, equipment rental and leasing, mailing, reproduction, and stenographic services. Other sales representatives work for firms that offer a wide range of other services, such as engineering and management, personal, amusement and recreation, automotive repair, membership organizations, hotels, motion pictures, health, and education services.

Qualifications and Training

Many employers require services sales representatives to have college degrees, but requirements may vary depending on the industry a particular company represents. Employers who market advertising services seek individuals with college degrees in advertising or marketing or master's degrees in business administration; companies that market educational services prefer individuals with advanced degrees in marketing or related fields.

Many hotels seek graduates from college hotel administration programs, and companies involved with selling computer services and telephone systems prefer sales representatives with computer science or engineering backgrounds. College courses in business, economics, communications, and marketing are helpful in obtaining other jobs as services sales representatives.

Employers may hire experienced, high-performing sales representatives who have only a high school diploma, and this is particularly true for those who sell nontechnical services, such as exterminating, laundry, or funeral services.

Many firms conduct intensive training programs for their sales representatives. A sound training program covers the history of the business; origin, development, and uses of the service; effective prospecting methods; presentation of the service; answering customer complaints; creating customer demand; closing a sale; writing an order; company policies; and using technical support personnel.

Sales representatives also may attend seminars on a wide range of subjects given by in-house or outside training institutions. These sessions acquaint employees with new services and products and help them maintain and update their sales techniques and may include motivational or sensitivity training to make sales representatives more effective in dealing with people. Sales staffs often receive training in the use of computers and communications technology in order to increase their productivity.

To be successful, sales representatives should be pleasant, outgoing, and have good rapport with people. They must be highly motivated, well organized, and efficient. Good grooming and a neat appearance are essential, as are self-confidence, reliability, and the ability to communicate effectively. Sales representatives should be self-starters who can work under pressure to meet sales goals. Those who have good sales records and leadership ability may advance to supervisory and managerial positions. Frequent contact with businesspeople in other firms provides sales workers with leads about job openings, enhancing opportunities for advancement.

Compensation

The median annual income for full-time advertising sales representatives is about $43,000. Earnings of representatives who sell technical services generally are higher than earnings of those who sell nontechnical services.

The average yearly income for technical services sales representatives, including commissions, is about $48,650 to $84,880 for senior sales staff.

Earnings of experienced sales representatives depend on performance. Successful sales representatives who establish a strong customer base can earn more than managers in their firms. Some sales representatives earn well over $100,000 a year.

Sales representatives work on different types of compensation plans. Some receive a straight salary; others are paid solely on a commission basis—a percentage of the dollar value of their sales. Most firms pay a combination of salary and commissions.

Some services sales representatives receive a base salary plus incentive pay that adds 50 to 70 percent to the base salary. In addition to the same benefits package received by other employees of the firm, outside sales representatives have expense accounts to cover meals and travel and, in some cases, a company car. Many employers offer bonuses—including vacation time, trips, and prizes—for sales that exceed company quotas.

In spite of all the perks, earnings may vary widely from year to year with fluctuating economic conditions and consumer and business expectations.

Manufacturing and Wholesale Sales

Articles of clothing, books, and computers are among the thousands of products bought and sold each day. Manufacturers' and wholesale sales representatives play an important role in this process. While retail sales workers sell products directly to customers, manufacturers' representatives market their products to other manufacturers, wholesale and retail establishments, government agencies, and other institutions. Regardless of the types of products they sell, the primary duties of these sales representatives are to interest wholesale and retail buyers and purchasing agents in their merchandise and ensure that any questions or concerns of current clients are addressed.

Sales representatives represent one manufacturer or several, or they may serve wholesale distributors by selling one product or a complimentary line of products. Sales representatives also advise their clients on methods to reduce costs, use their products, and increase sales. They market their company's products to manufacturers, wholesale and retail establishments, construction contractors, government agencies, and other institutions.

Depending on where they work, sales representatives have different job titles. Those employed directly by a manufacturer or wholesaler often are called sales representatives. Manufacturers' agents or manufacturers' representatives are self-employed sales workers or independent firms who contract their services to all types of manufacturing companies. However, many of these titles are used interchangeably.

Sales representatives spend much of their time traveling to meet with prospective buyers and current clients. During a sales call, they discuss the client's needs and suggest how their merchandise or services can meet those needs. They may show samples or catalogs that describe items their company stocks and inform customers about prices, availability, and ways in which their products can save money and improve productivity. Because a vast number of manufacturers and wholesalers sell similar products, sales representatives must emphasize any unique qualities of their products and services.

Manufacturers' agents or manufacturers' representatives might sell several complementary products made by different manufacturers and, thus, take a broad approach to their customers' businesses. Sales representatives may help install new equipment and train employees. They also take orders and resolve any problems with or complaints about the merchandise.

Obtaining new accounts is an important part of the job. Sales representatives follow leads from other clients, track advertisements in trade journals, participate in trade shows and conferences, and may visit potential clients unannounced. In addition, they may spend time meeting with and entertaining prospective clients during evenings and weekends.

In a process that can take several months, sales representatives present their product and negotiate the sale. Aided by a laptop computer connected to the Internet, they often can answer technical and nontechnical questions immediately.

Frequently, sales representatives who lack technical expertise work as a team with a technical expert. In this arrangement, the technical expert will attend the sales presentation to explain the product and answer questions or concerns. The sales representative makes the preliminary contact with customers, introduces the company's product, and closes the sale. The representative is then able to spend more time maintaining and soliciting accounts and less time acquiring technical knowledge. After the sale, representatives may make follow-up visits to ensure that the equipment is functioning properly. They may even help train the customers' employees in operating and maintaining the equipment. Those selling consumer goods often suggest how and where merchandise should be displayed. Working with retailers, they may help arrange promotional programs, store displays, and advertising.

Sales representatives have several duties beyond selling products. They also analyze sales statistics; prepare reports; and handle administrative duties, such as filing their expense account reports, scheduling appointments, and making travel plans. They study literature about new and existing products and monitor the sales, prices, and products of their competitors.

Manufacturers' agents who operate a sales agency must also manage their business. This requires organizational and general business skills, as well as knowledge of accounting, marketing, and administration.

Sales Managers

Sales managers direct the firm's sales programs. They assign sales territories and goals and establish training programs for their sales representatives. Managers advise their sales representatives on ways to improve performance. In large, multiproduct firms, they oversee regional and local sales managers and their staffs.

Managers maintain contact with dealers and distributors. They analyze sales statistics gathered by the sales staff to determine sales potential and inventory requirements and monitor the preferences of customers, information that is vital to develop new products and maximize profits.

Sales managers must go out in the field to see their sales reps, who can't afford to take the time to travel to the office and risk losing sales. They make sure the reps are using the right techniques and handling each situation the way it should be handled in order to get the maximum sales volume.

Qualifications and Training

The background needed for sales jobs varies by product line and market. Many employers hire individuals with previous sales experience who do not have a college degree but often prefer those with some college education. The increase in technical and analytical aspects of many products has led more employers to prefer candidates with a bachelor's degree. Nevertheless, for some consumer products, factors such as sales ability, personality, and familiarity with brands and products are more important than educational background. On the other hand, firms selling complex, technical products may require a technical degree in addition to some sales experience.

Many sales representatives attend seminars in sales techniques or take courses in marketing, economics, communication, or even a foreign language to provide the extra edge needed to make sales.

In general, companies are looking for the best and brightest individuals who have the personality and desire to sell. Sales representatives need to be familiar with computer technology as computers are increasingly used in the workplace to enter and track orders and to monitor inventory levels.

Many companies have formal training programs for beginning sales representatives lasting up to two years. However, most businesses are accelerating these programs to reduce costs and expedite the returns from training. In some programs, trainees rotate among jobs in plants and offices to learn all phases of production, installation, and distribution of the product. In others, trainees take formal classroom instruction at the plant, followed by on-the-job training under the supervision of a field sales manager.

New workers may get training by accompanying experienced workers on their sales calls. As they gain familiarity with the firm's products and clients, these workers are given increasing responsibility until they are eventually assigned their own territory. As businesses experience greater competition, increased pressure is placed upon sales representatives to produce sales.

Sales representatives stay abreast of new products and the changing needs of their customers in a variety of ways. They attend trade shows at which new products and technologies are showcased. They also attend conferences and conventions to meet other sales representatives and clients and discuss new product developments. In addition, the entire sales force may participate in company-sponsored meetings to review sales performance, product development, sales goals, and profitability.

Those who want to become sales representatives should be goal oriented and persuasive and work well both independently and as part of a team. A pleasant personality and appearance, the ability to communicate well with people, and problem-solving skills are highly valued. Furthermore, completing a sale can take several months and thus requires patience and perseverance.

Frequently, promotion takes the form of an assignment to a larger account or territory where commissions are likely to be greater. Experienced sales representatives may move into jobs as sales trainers, instructing new employees on sales techniques and company policies. Those who have good sales records and leadership ability may advance to higher-level positions, such as sales supervisor, district manager, or vice president of sales.

In addition to advancement opportunities within a firm, some manufacturers' agents go into business for themselves. Others find opportunities in purchasing, advertising, or marketing research.

Compensation

Compensation methods vary significantly by the type of firm and product sold. Most employers use a combination of salary and commission or salary plus bonus. Commissions usually are based on the number of sales, whereas bonuses may depend on individual performance, on the performance of all sales workers in the group or district, or on the company's performance.

Median annual earnings in the industries employing the largest numbers of sales representatives, technical and scientific products, in 2002 were as follows:

Wholesale electronic markets and agents and brokers	$64,070
Professional and commercial equipment and supplies merchant wholesalers	$60,890
Drugs and druggists' sundries merchant wholesalers	$57,890
Machinery, equipment, and supplies merchant wholesalers	$53,140
Electrical and electronic goods merchant wholesalers	$50,550

Median annual earnings of sales representatives, wholesale and manufacturing, technical and scientific products, were $55,740, including commission, in 2002. The middle 50 percent earned between $39,480 and $79,380 a year. The lowest 10 percent earned less than $28,770, and the highest 10 percent earned more than $108,010 a year.

Median annual earnings of sales representatives, wholesale and manufacturing, except technical and scientific products, were $42,730, including commission, in 2002. The middle 50 percent earned between $30,660 and $60,970 a year. The lowest 10 percent earned less than $22,610, and the highest 10 percent earned more than $88,990 a year.

Median annual earnings in the industries employing the largest numbers of sales representatives, except technical and scientific products, in 2002 were as follows:

Wholesale electronic markets and agents and brokers	$48,320
Machinery, equipment, and supplies merchant wholesalers	$44,030
Professional and commercial equipment and supplies merchant wholesalers	$43,880
Grocery and related product wholesalers	$41,840
Miscellaneous nondurable goods merchant wholesalers	$37,940

In addition to their earnings, sales representatives usually are reimbursed for expenses such as transportation costs, meals, hotels, and entertaining customers. They often receive benefits such as health and life insurance, pension plan, vacation and sick leave, personal use of a company car, and frequent-flyer mileage. Some companies offer incentives such as free vacation trips or gifts for outstanding sales workers.

Unlike those working directly for a manufacturer or wholesaler, manufacturers' agents are paid strictly on commission and usually are not reimbursed for expenses. Depending on the type of product or products they are selling, their experience in the field, and the number of clients, their earnings can be significantly higher or lower than those working in direct sales.

Words from the Pros

Read the personal accounts of the following sales professionals to
see whether a career in sales might be right for you.

Marty Gorelick, Sales Professional

Marty Gorelick has a bachelor of arts degree from Long Island
University in Brooklyn, New York, and more than a dozen years of
experience in computer hardware sales. He has attended seminars
from all of the major computer manufacturers: Compaq, IBM,
Hewlett-Packard, Sony, Apple, and NEC. Marty is the account
manager for county government sales at GE Capital IT Solutions
in Miami, Florida, where he services Metro-Dade, Broward, and
Pasco Counties, plus all cities, towns, and villages within these
municipalities.

"The computer industry is constantly changing," he says. "It is
the fastest-growing industry in the world. Computers have made
communications possible at lightning speed."

Marty cites advances in science, medicine, engineering, law,
manufacturing, and education as just some examples of the
ways in which computers have changed industry and society. All
of these technological advances make his job that much more
challenging.

"A typical day for me begins when I arrive at my office about
6:30 A.M.," Marty says. "After running the branch's allocation
reports for all the salespeople in our office, I check my voice mail
for any emergency issues that must be addressed quickly. An
example might be a critical shipment that hasn't arrived on time
or a file server that has developed a problem and is inoperable.
These situations demand my immediate attention.

"I read my e-mail messages next. It's not unusual to have
between five and fifteen messages ranging from company updates
to manufacturer price changes to additions and deletions from

any number of vendors. Some messages require a response ASAP; others can be addressed during my regular business day.

"Next stop is my in-box, which usually contains a collection of faxes that have arrived since I left the office at the end of business yesterday. These faxes could contain purchase orders, manufacturer promotional notices, seminar information, or news of a prospective customer looking for a great reseller like ours! All this, and the clock has not yet struck 8 A.M."

Once the official business day begins, Marty handles calls from customers concerning products, services, and orders. A typical day might include a quick staff meeting to discuss changes in plans or a new company procedure. Afternoons are spent finishing projects, faxing price quotes, and filing purchase orders and invoices.

In addition to the regular routine, Marty also puts out a special electronic price list every sixty days, which reflects the constantly changing prices. This process usually takes three to four working days. He also provides a manuscript of five thousand or more items from a third-party vendor. On any given day, he might also accompany a manufacturer to a client facility, where they will call on any number of departments that have requested information or a demonstration of a new item.

"My day ends about the time that local traffic starts to build on the highway," Marty says. "This represents a ten-plus-hour day, five days a week, four-point-three weeks a month. To say this is a hectic day is putting it mildly. However, if you enjoy what you do, it can be and is a labor of love.

"The most enjoyable part of my position is helping my customers understand their needs in respect to the use of the equipment," Marty says. "An example would be a customer interested in a laptop computer to do presentations at remote sites versus a client needing a laptop for communicating to his home base.

"The upside of my business is the satisfaction of being productive and helping others do the same. When I complete a project with confidence in a timely manner so my customers can enjoy productivity, I take a moment to sit back and breathe easy."

Marty also talks about the downsides of his career. "If I had to pick a project I least like to perform, it's the tons of paperwork that is a necessary evil in the day-to-day flow of business.

"Another downside is always being in a race with the clock. I try never to let the clock win. I also refuse to let a discontinued product stop me from saying to customers that I can fill their needs. Somewhere out there is a replacement part. All salespeople are part detective. We look until we find what we need to help our customers."

Marty Gorelick offers some advice for anyone interested in a career in computer sales. "For those who are considering entering my world, I would say to be prepared to plan for a very exciting career. Technology advances as fast as you can absorb yesterday's breakthroughs. Pick a school that offers the career path that you wish to follow (sales and marketing, computer network engineering, or service and repair). Attend as many seminars in the field as possible. Read as many journals that pertain to your area of interest. Spend as much time as you can afford talking to those around you in that particular field. Don't be afraid to roll up your sleeves and get your hands dirty. Ask a million questions. Experiment with the knowledge you've gained. Share your findings with others and always remember that, to achieve success, you must make learning a lifelong endeavor."

Donna Maas, Business Owner and Sales Professional

Donna Maas's formal studies include interior architecture, design, drafting, and oil painting. With a background in graphic art, she designs all marketing materials and packaging for MAAS Polishing Systems of Willowbrook, Illinois. She serves as president and CEO of the company.

After six years of using various cleaning and polishing products and always wishing for something better, Maas asked a chemist to assist her in formulating a product that worked. The end result is MAAS Polishing Creme, a product that quickly restores all metals, fiberglass, Plexiglas, and dull oxidized paintwork to an unusually brilliant finish. "Little did I realize how this innovative formula would revolutionize the polishing-products industry," she says.

"The job is glamorous, hectic, and unpredictable," Donna explains. "My role encompasses product development, designing marketing materials, and fielding calls from major retailers while maintaining balance in the offices, warehouse, and factory. This, combined with extensive traveling and television appearances on QVC to demonstrate my products, requires tremendous stamina. Everyone within the company, from my executive assistant to the shipping department, will tell you that every project I tackle must be treated with urgency, requiring immediate attention. This keeps my office personnel (including myself) operating at an unusually fast pace."

Hard work paid off for Donna. By her third year in business, she experienced an 800 percent growth on her initial investment. "It is tremendously fulfilling to obtain such rapid success and world-wide recognition," Donna says. "I would have to think long and hard if asked what the downside of my career is because I can't think of anything!"

Based on her experience, Donna Maas offers some advice for aspiring business owners. "I would advise others who wish to get into this field to stay focused. The most difficult thing for an entrepreneur to do is to focus. You have so many things coming at you all at once. I have learned to concentrate on the most promising opportunities. When you become scattered and attempt to address every opportunity, your success is hindered."

Jim LeClair, Business Owner and Sales Professional

Jim LeClair is the owner and sales manager for Advanced Computer Services in Lawrence, Kansas. He earned a high school diploma and took some secondary accounting and business classes. He also has engaged in ongoing seminars and classes that are offered by suppliers to enhance sales, technical training, and product knowledge.

"I was burned out on retail and on working for others," he says, "so my wife and I decided to form our own business. She had a strong computer background, and I had more of the business background. We felt our strengths would complement one another. Our company consists of training and network installations, network design to integration, support, and fiber optics, to name a few."

Jim's business employs five people who work Monday through Friday from 8 A.M. until 5 P.M. He strives to maintain a relaxed yet professional atmosphere, being mindful of employees' needs and working to keep morale as high as possible.

A typical day in Jim's business is difficult to describe, since things can change on short notice. Jim arrives at work at 7 A.M. and stays until 7 P.M. He spends about 30 percent of his time handling customers' needs, 40 percent working on sales, and 30 percent on the daily activities involved in running the business.

Jim says, "What I like best is seeing how happy the customer is when we say, 'This is how the network will work,' and then the network performs as well or better than we anticipated. What I like least is having to discipline employees or contemplate lost sales.

"To be successful in this kind of work, it's very important to keep abreast of the current technology at all times, to be a good listener, to be flexible, to be able to read people, and to understand what they really want, not what they say they want. You have to be able to think quickly on your feet and have a semiaggressive nature. You just can't take no for an answer. Still, you must sell the customers what they want. Don't try to sell people something that isn't right for them just because you can make some money."

Jim's advice to anyone interested in a similar career is based on basic personal traits. He says, "I'd advise those who are considering computer sales to be honest, to be fair, and always to do a good job. Our business has grown because we have gained the trust of both our customers and our employees."

For More Information

By contacting the following professional associations, you can obtain more information about each category of sales.

Retail Sales

Information on careers in retail sales may be obtained from the personnel offices of local stores, from state merchants' associations, or from local unions of the United Food and Commercial Workers International Union (www.ufcw.org).

General information about retailing is available from:

National Retail Federation
375 Seventh Street NW, Suite 1100
Washington, DC 20004
www.nrf.com

Service Sales

For details about employment opportunities for service sales representatives, contact employers who sell services in your area.

For information on careers and scholarships in hotel management and sales contact:

The American Hotel and Lodging Association (AH&LA)
Information Center
1201 New York Avenue NW, Suite 600
Washington, DC 20005
www.ahla.com

Manufacturing and Wholesale Sales

Information on manufacturers' agents is available from:

Sales and Marketing Executives International
PO Box 1390
Sumas, WA 98295
www.smei.org

CHAPTER FIVE

Careers in Insurance, Real Estate, and Travel Sales

We think of settings for sales professions as retail, service, and wholesale markets. While it might seem less apparent, the professionals we consult when we need insurance, want to buy or sell a home, or plan a vacation are also involved in sales. In this chapter we look at these three professions to see what is involved in this aspect of the sales industry.

Insurance Sales

The insurance industry consists mainly of insurance carriers, insurance agencies, and brokerages. In general, insurance carriers are large companies that provide insurance and assume the risks covered by the policy. Insurance agencies and brokerages sell insurance policies for the carriers.

Some agencies and brokerages are directly affiliated with a particular insurer and sell only that carrier's policies, but many are independent and are thus free to market the policies of a variety of insurance carriers.

Insurance Agents

Is your car sufficiently insured? Is the policy easy for you to understand? If you are not sure about the answers to these questions, then you need an insurance agent.

Most people have their first contact with an insurance company through an insurance sales agent, who acts as a liaison between the company and the insured party. These workers help individuals, families, and businesses select insurance policies that provide the best protection for their lives, health, and property. Insurance sales agents who work exclusively for one insurance company are referred to as captive agents. Independent insurance agents, or brokers, represent several companies and place insurance policies for their clients with the company that offers the best rate and coverage. In either case, agents prepare reports, maintain records, seek out new clients, and, in the event of a loss, help policyholders settle their insurance claims. Increasingly, some are also offering their clients financial analysis or advice on ways the clients can minimize risk.

Insurance sales agents, commonly referred to as producers in the insurance industry, sell one or more types of insurance, such as property and casualty, life, health, disability, and long-term care.

Property and casualty insurance agents sell policies that protect individuals and businesses from financial loss resulting from automobile accidents, fire, theft, storms, and other events that can damage property. For businesses, property and casualty insurance can also cover injured workers' compensation, product liability claims, or medical malpractice claims.

Life insurance agents specialize in selling policies that pay beneficiaries when a policyholder dies. Depending on the policyholder's circumstances, a cash-value policy can be designed to provide retirement income, funds for the education of children, or other benefits. Life insurance agents also sell annuities that promise a retirement income.

Health insurance agents sell insurance policies that cover the costs of medical care and loss of income due to illness or injury. They also may sell dental insurance and short- and long-term-disability insurance policies.

An increasing number of insurance sales agents are offering comprehensive financial planning services to their clients, such as retirement planning, estate planning, or assistance in setting up pension plans for businesses. As a result, many insurance agents are involved in cross-selling or total account development. Besides offering insurance, these agents may become licensed to sell mutual funds, variable annuities, and other securities. This practice is most common with life insurance agents who already sell annuities; however, property and casualty agents also sell financial products.

Technology has greatly affected the insurance industry, making it much more efficient and giving the agent the ability to take on more clients. Agents' computers are now linked directly to insurance carriers via the Internet, making the tasks of obtaining price quotes and processing applications and service requests faster and easier. Computers also allow agents to be better informed about new products that the insurance carriers may be offering.

The growth of the Internet in the insurance industry is gradually altering the relationship between agent and client. In the past, agents devoted much of their time to marketing and selling products to new clients, a practice that is now changing. Increasingly, clients are obtaining insurance quotes from a company's website and then contacting the company directly to purchase policies. This interaction gives the client a more active role in selecting a policy at the best price while reducing the amount of time agents spend actively seeking new clients.

Because insurance sales agents also obtain many new accounts through referrals, it is important that they maintain regular contact with their clients to ensure that the clients' financial needs are being met. Developing a satisfied clientele that will recommend an agent's services to other potential customers is a key to success in this field.

Working Conditions

Most insurance sales agents are based in small offices, from which they contact clients and provide information on the policies they sell. However, much of their time may be spent outside their offices, traveling locally to meet with clients, close sales, or investigate claims. In these situations, agents usually determine their own hours of work and often schedule evening and weekend appointments for the convenience of clients. Although most agents work a forty-hour week, some work sixty hours a week or longer. Commercial sales agents, in particular, may meet with clients during business hours and then spend evenings doing paperwork and preparing presentations to prospective clients.

Qualifications and Training

For insurance sales agent jobs, most companies and independent agencies prefer to hire college graduates, especially those who have majored in business or economics. High school graduates are occasionally hired if they have proven sales ability or have been successful in other types of work.

In fact, many entrants to insurance sales agent jobs transfer from other occupations. In selling commercial insurance, technical experience in a particular field can help sell policies to those in the same profession. As a result, new agents tend to be older than entrants in many other occupations.

College training may help agents grasp the technical aspects of insurance policies and the fundamentals and procedures of selling insurance. Many colleges and universities offer courses in insurance, and a few schools offer a bachelor's degree in the field. College courses in finance, mathematics, accounting, economics, business law, marketing, and business administration enable insurance sales agents to understand how social and economic conditions relate to the insurance industry. Courses in psychology, sociology, and public speaking can prove useful in improving sales techniques. In addition, because computers provide instantaneous information on a wide variety of financial products and greatly improve agents' efficiency, familiarity with computers and popular software packages has become very important.

Insurance sales agents must obtain a license in the states where they plan to do business. Separate licenses are required for agents to sell life and health insurance and property and casualty insurance. In most states, licenses are issued only to applicants who complete specified prelicensing courses and who pass state examinations covering insurance fundamentals and state insurance laws. As a result of the Gramm-Leach-Bliley Act of 1999, the industry is increasingly moving toward uniform state licensing standards and reciprocal licensing, allowing agents who earn a license in one state to become licensed in other states upon passing the appropriate courses and examination.

A number of organizations offer professional designation programs that certify one's expertise in specialties such as life, health, and property and casualty insurance, as well as financial consulting. Although voluntary, such programs assure both clients and employers that an agent has gained a thorough understanding of the relevant specialty. Agents are usually required to complete a specified number of hours of continuing education to retain their designation.

Getting Ahead

As the diversity of financial products sold by insurance agents increases, more employers are placing greater emphasis on continuing professional education. It is important for agents to keep up-to-date on issues concerning clients. Changes in tax laws, government benefits programs, and other state and federal regulations can affect the insurance needs of clients and the way in which agents conduct business.

Agents can enhance their selling skills and broaden their knowledge of insurance and other financial services by taking courses at colleges and universities and by attending institutes, conferences, and seminars sponsored by insurance organizations. Most state licensing authorities also have mandatory continuing education requirements focusing on insurance laws, consumer protection, and the technical details of various insurance policies.

As the demand for financial products and financial planning increases, many insurance agents are choosing to gain the proper licensing and certification to sell securities and other financial products. Doing so, however, requires substantial study and passing an additional examination—either the Series 6 or Series 7 licensing exam, both of which are administered by the National Association of Securities Dealers (NASD). The Series 6 exam is for individuals who wish to sell only mutual funds and variable annuities, whereas the Series 7 exam is the main NASD series license that qualifies agents as general securities sales representatives. In addition, to further demonstrate competency in the area of financial planning, many agents find it worthwhile to earn the designation Certified Financial Planner or Chartered Financial Consultant.

Insurance sales agents should be flexible, enthusiastic, confident, disciplined, hard working, and willing to solve problems. They should communicate effectively and inspire customer confidence. Because they usually work without supervision, sales agents must be able to plan their time well and have the initiative to locate new clients.

An insurance sales agent who shows ability and leadership may become a sales manager in a local office. A few advance to agency superintendent or executive positions. However, many who have built up a good clientele prefer to remain in sales work. Some agents, particularly in the property and casualty field, establish their own independent agencies or brokerage firms.

Training for Insurance Agents in Canada

Entry into insurance sales usually requires at least secondary school graduation and completion of provincial licensing requirements. Graduation from a college or university program in business administration or financial management or a bachelor's degree in an area of arts or science is often an asset.

On-the-job training and insurance industry courses and training programs are standard requirements. In addition, licensing by the insurance governing body in the province or territory of employment is required.

Compensation

The median annual earnings of wage and salary insurance sales agents were $40,750 in 2002. The middle 50 percent earned between $28,860 and $64,450. The lowest 10 percent had earnings of $21,730 or less, while the highest 10 percent earned more than $101,460. Median annual earnings in 2002 in the two industries employing the largest number of insurance sales agents were $40,480 for insurance agencies, brokerages, and other insurance-related activities and $42,130 for insurance carriers.

Many independent agents are paid by commission alone, whereas sales workers who are employees of an agency or an insurance carrier may be paid in one of three ways: salary only, salary plus commission, or salary plus bonus. In general, commissions are the most common form of compensation, especially for experienced agents. The amount of the commission depends on the type and amount of insurance sold and on whether the transaction is a new policy or a renewal. Bonuses usually are awarded when agents meet their sales goals or when an agency meets its profit goals. Some agents involved with financial planning receive a fee for their services, rather than a commission.

Company-paid benefits to insurance sales agents usually include continuing education, training to qualify for licensing, group insurance plans, office space, and clerical support services. Some companies also may pay for automobile and transportation expenses, attendance at conventions and meetings, promotion and marketing expenses, and retirement plans. Independent agents working for insurance agencies receive fewer benefits, but their commissions may be higher to help them pay for marketing and other expenses.

Real Estate Sales

Do the terms *EIK*, *CAC*, and *W/D* mean anything to you? If you are buying or selling a home, you need to know that they mean eat-in-kitchen, central air conditioning, and washer/dryer. Since real estate transactions are not only among the most important financial events in peoples' lives but also among the most complex legal transactions, many people seek the expertise of a professional for this important event.

Real estate agents and brokers need to have a thorough knowledge of the housing market in their communities. They must know which neighborhoods will best fit their clients' needs and budgets. They have to be familiar with local zoning and tax laws and know how and where to obtain financing.

Agents and brokers also act as intermediaries for price negotiations between buyer and seller.

Real Estate Brokers

Brokers are independent businesspeople who, for a fee, sell real estate owned by others. They may also rent and manage properties. They also arrange for title searches and for meetings between buyers and sellers when details of the transactions are agreed upon and the new owners take possession.

In closing sales, brokers often provide buyers with information on loans to finance their purchases. A broker's knowledge, resourcefulness, and creativity in arranging financing that is most favorable to the prospective buyer often mean the difference between success and failure in closing a sale.

In some cases, brokers or agents assume the responsibilities in closing sales, but, in many areas, this is done by lawyers, lenders, or title companies. Brokers also manage their own offices, supervise associate agents, advertise properties, and handle other business matters.

Real Estate Agents

Real estate agents generally are independent sales workers who provide their services to a licensed broker on a contract basis. In return, the broker pays the agent a portion of the commission earned from property sold through the firm by the agent. Today, relatively few agents receive salaries as employees of a broker or realty firm. Instead, most derive their incomes solely from commissions.

Responsibilities of Real Estate Professionals

Most real estate brokers and sales agents sell residential property. A small number, usually employed in large or specialized firms, sell commercial, industrial, agricultural, or other types of real estate.

Every specialty requires knowledge of that particular type of property and clientele. For example, selling or leasing business property requires an understanding of leasing practices, business trends, and the location of the property. Agents who sell or lease industrial properties must know about the region's transportation, utilities, and labor supply. Whatever the type of property, the agent or broker must know how to meet the client's particular requirements.

Before showing residential properties to potential buyers, agents meet with them to get a feeling for the type of home the buyers would like. In this prequalifying phase, the agent determines how much the buyers can afford to spend. In addition, the agent and the buyer usually sign a loyalty contract, often called an exclusive, which states the agent will be the only one to show houses to the buyers.

An agent or broker uses a computer to generate lists of properties for sale, their location and description, and available sources of financing. In some cases, agents and brokers use computers to give buyers a virtual tour of properties in which they are interested. With a computer, buyers can view interior and exterior images or floor plans without leaving the real estate office.

Agents may meet several times with prospective buyers to discuss and visit available properties, identifying and emphasizing the most pertinent selling points. To a young family looking for a house, they may stress the convenient floor plan, the area's low crime rate, or the proximity to schools and shopping centers. To a potential investor, they may point out the tax advantages of owning a rental property or the ease of finding a renter. If bargaining over price becomes necessary, agents must follow their client's instructions carefully and may have to present counteroffers in order to get the best possible price.

Once the buyer and seller have signed a contract, the real estate broker or agent must make sure that all special terms of the contract are met before the closing date. For example, the agent must make sure that the mandated and agreed-upon inspections—including home, termite, and radon inspections—take place. Also, if the seller agrees to any repairs, the broker or agent must see that they are made. Increasingly, brokers and agents are handling environmental problems as well by making sure that the properties they sell meet environmental regulations. For example, they may be responsible for dealing with lead paint on the walls. While loan officers, attorneys, or other persons handle many details, the agent must ensure that they are completed.

Qualifications and Training

Real estate brokers and sales agents must be licensed in every state and the District of Columbia. Prospective agents must be high school graduates, at least eighteen years old, and pass a written test. The examination—more comprehensive for brokers than for agents—includes questions on basic real estate transactions and laws affecting the sale of property. Most states require candidates for the general sales license to complete between thirty and ninety hours of classroom instruction. Those seeking a broker's license need between sixty and ninety hours of formal training and a specific amount of experience selling real estate, usually one to three years. Some states waive the experience requirements for the broker's license for applicants who have a bachelor's degree in real estate.

State licenses typically must be renewed every one or two years, usually without having to take an examination. However, many states require continuing education for license renewals. Prospective agents and brokers should contact the real estate licensing commission of the state in which they wish to work in order to verify exact licensing requirements.

As real estate transactions have become more legally complex, many firms have turned to college graduates to fill positions. A large number of agents and brokers have some college training. College courses in real estate, finance, business administration, statistics, economics, law, and English are helpful. For those who intend to start their own company, business courses such as marketing and accounting are as important as those in real estate or finance.

Personality traits are as vital as academic background. Brokers look for applicants who possess a pleasant personality, are honest, and present a neat appearance. Maturity, tact, trustworthiness, and enthusiasm for the job are required in order to motivate prospective customers in this highly competitive field. Agents should be well organized, be detail oriented, and have a good memory for names, faces, and business particulars.

Those interested in jobs as real estate agents often begin in their own communities, since knowledge of local neighborhoods is a clear advantage. Under the direction of an experienced agent, beginners learn the practical aspects of the job, including the use of computers to locate or list available properties and identify sources of financing.

Many firms offer formal training programs for both beginners and experienced agents. Larger firms usually offer more extensive programs than smaller firms. More than a thousand universities, colleges, and junior colleges offer courses in real estate. At some, a student can earn an associate's or bachelor's degree with a major in real estate; several offer advanced degrees.

Many local real estate associations that are members of the National Association of Realtors sponsor courses covering the fundamentals and legal aspects of the field. Advanced courses in mortgage financing, property development and management, and other subjects also are available through various affiliates of the National Association of Realtors.

Getting Ahead

Advancement opportunities for agents usually take the form of higher rates of commission. As agents gain knowledge and expertise, they become more efficient in closing a greater number of transactions and increase their earnings.

In many large firms, experienced agents can advance to sales manager or general manager. Those who have earned a broker's license may open their own offices. Others with experience and training in estimating property value may become real estate appraisers, and people familiar with operating and maintaining rental properties may become property managers.

Experienced agents and brokers with a thorough knowledge of business conditions and property values in their localities may enter mortgage financing or real estate investment counseling.

Training for Real Estate Agents in Canada

According to the Canadian Real Estate Association, education and licensing requirements for jobs in the real estate industry are established by the individual provinces. Aspiring agents and brokers should check the requirements of the province in which they intend to sell real estate.

In most provinces, educational requirements must be met before one can enter the field. A period of supervised practical training, sometimes called "articling," may also be required before a worker can be registered as a real estate professional.

Colleges and universities offer a variety of real estate or related courses. At many of these colleges, students can specialize in a program that leads to a bachelor's degree in real estate. Some universities offer graduate-level courses. Continuing education is also required in many provinces, so that real estate professionals can stay current on the issues that affect the industry.

Provincial licensing is required throughout the country. Although licensing requirements vary, all provinces and territories require prospective salespeople and brokers to pass a written exam. Information on licensing can be obtained from the real estate association of each province.

Compensation

The median annual earnings of salaried real estate agents, including commissions, were $30,930 in 2002. The middle 50 percent earned between $21,010 and $52,860 a year. The lowest 10 percent earned less than $15,480, and the highest 10 percent earned more than $83,780.

Median annual earnings of salaried real estate brokers, including commission, were $50,330 in 2002. The middle 50 percent earned between $29,240 and $90,170 a year. The lowest 10 percent earned less than $17,920, and the highest 10 percent earned more than $145,600 a year.

Commissions on sales are the main source of earnings of real estate agents and brokers. The rate of commission varies according to whatever the agent and broker agree on, the type of property, and its value. The percentage paid on the sale of farm and commercial properties or unimproved land usually is higher than the percentage paid for selling a home.

Commissions may be divided among several agents and brokers. When the property is sold, the broker or agent who obtained the listing usually shares the commission with the broker or agent who made the sale and with the selling agent's the firm. Although an agent's share varies greatly from one firm to another, often it is about half of the total amount received by the firm. Agents who both list and sell a property maximize their commission.

Income usually increases as an agent gains experience, but individual ability, economic conditions, and the type and location of the property also affect earnings. Sales workers who are active in community organizations and in local real estate associations can broaden their contacts and increase their earnings. A beginner's earnings often are irregular, because a few weeks or even months may go by without a sale. Although some brokers allow an agent to draw against future earnings from a special account, the practice is not usual with new employees. The beginner, therefore, should have enough money to live for about six months or until commissions increase.

The Downsides

In addition to lean income periods, sometimes a deal can fall through at the last minute. For example, buyers might be prequalified for a mortgage, based on their income, amount of debt, and other factors. But another financial examination is conducted just before closing. If the buyers have purchased new furniture, for example, or in some other way changed their financial picture, it can kill the deal.

Agents also have to be very careful when dealing with new clients who are strangers. This is especially true for female realtors. Brokers will encourage their agents to work in pairs if possible and always to arrange the first meeting with the client to take place at the office, not at the property. Another precaution an agent can take is to have the client follow in his own car, rather than ride to a property in the agent's vehicle.

There are many times when you show a client twenty properties and you don't sell a thing. You can spend a lot of time, but most agents don't look at it as wasted time. It gives you a chance to increase your knowledge of different properties new to the market. You can always use that information for the next call.

Agents and brokers often work more than a standard forty-hour week. They usually work evenings and weekends and are always on call to suit the needs of clients. Business usually is slower during the winter season. Although the hours are long and frequently irregular, most agents and brokers have the freedom to determine their own schedules. Consequently, they can arrange their work so they can have time off when they want it.

Travel Sales

Out of all the industries worldwide, travel and tourism continue to grow at an astounding rate. In fact, according to the Travel Works for America Council, it is the second-largest employer in the United States (the first being health services). Nearly everyone tries to take at least one vacation every year, and many people travel frequently on business. Some travel for education or for a special honeymoon or anniversary trip.

Constantly changing airfares and schedules, thousands of available vacation packages, and a vast amount of travel information on the Internet can make travel planning frustrating and time consuming. To sort out the many travel options, tourists and businesspeople often turn to travel agents, who assess their needs and help them make the best possible travel arrangements. Also, many major cruise lines, resorts, and specialty travel groups use travel agents to promote travel packages to millions of people every year.

In general, travel agents give advice on destinations and make arrangements for transportation, hotel accommodations, car rentals, tours, and recreation. They also may advise on weather conditions, restaurants, tourist attractions, and recreation. For international travel, agents also provide information on customs regulations, required papers (passports, visas, and certificates of vaccination), and currency exchange rates.

Travel agents consult a variety of published and computer-based sources for information on departure and arrival times, fares, hotel ratings, and other accommodations. They may visit hotels, resorts, and restaurants to evaluate comfort, cleanliness, and quality of food and service so that they can base recommendations on their own travel experiences or those of colleagues or clients.

Travel agents also promote their services, using telemarketing, direct mail, and the Internet. They make presentations to social and special-interest groups, arrange advertising displays, and suggest company-sponsored trips to business managers. Depending on the size of the travel agency, an agent may specialize by type of travel, such as leisure or business, or destination, such as Europe or Africa.

Working Conditions

Travel agents spend most of their time behind a desk conferring with clients, completing paperwork, contacting airlines and hotels for travel arrangements, and promoting group tours. During vacation seasons and holiday periods, they may be under a great deal of pressure. Many agents, especially those who are self-employed, frequently work long hours. With advanced computer systems and telecommunication networks, some travel agents are able to work at home.

Qualifications and Training

The minimum requirement for working as a travel agent is a high school diploma or equivalent. Technology and computerization are having a profound effect on the work of travel agents, however, and formal or specialized training is increasingly important. Many vocational schools offer full-time travel agent programs that last several months, as well as evening and weekend programs. Travel agent courses also are offered in public adult education programs and in community and four-year colleges. A few colleges offer bachelor's or master's degrees in travel and tourism.

Although few college courses relate directly to the travel industry, a college education sometimes is desired by employers to establish a background in fields such as computer science, geography, communication, foreign languages, and world history. Courses in accounting and business management also are important, especially for those who expect to manage or start their own travel agencies.

The American Society of Travel Agents (ASTA) offers a correspondence course that provides a basic understanding of the travel industry. Travel agencies also provide on-the-job training for their employees, a significant part of which consists of computer instruction. All employers require computer skills of workers whose jobs involve the operation of airline and centralized reservation systems.

Experienced travel agents can take advanced self-study or group-study courses from the Travel Institute that lead to the Certified Travel Counselor (CTC) designation. The Travel Institute also offers marketing and sales skills development programs and destination specialist programs, which provide a detailed knowledge of regions such as North America, Western Europe, the Caribbean, and the Pacific Rim.

Personal travel experience or experience as an airline reservation agent is an asset because knowledge about a city or foreign country often helps to influence a client's travel plans. Patience and the ability to gain the confidence of clients also are useful qualities. Travel agents must be organized, accurate, and meticulous to compile information from various sources and plan and organize their clients' travel itineraries.

As the Internet has become an important tool for making travel arrangements, more travel agencies are using websites to provide their services to clients. This trend has increased the importance of computer skills in this occupation. Other desirable qualifications include good writing, interpersonal, and sales skills.

Some employees start as reservation clerks or receptionists in travel agencies. With experience and some formal training, they can take on greater responsibilities and eventually assume travel agent duties. In agencies with many offices, travel agents may advance to office manager or to other managerial positions.

Those who start their own agencies generally have had experience in an established agency. Before they can receive commissions, these agents usually must gain formal approval from suppliers or corporations, such as airlines, ship lines, or rail lines. The Airlines Reporting Corporation and the International Airlines Travel Agency Network, for example, are the approving bodies for airlines. To gain approval, an agency must be financially sound and employ at least one experienced manager or travel agent.

There are no federal licensing requirements for travel agents. However, nine states—California, Florida, Hawaii, Illinois, Iowa, Ohio, Oregon, Rhode Island, and Washington—require some form of registration or certification of retail sellers of travel services. More information may be obtained by contacting the office of the attorney general or the state's Department of Commerce.

Compensation

Experience, sales ability, and the size and location of the agency determine the salary of a travel agent. Median annual earnings of travel agents were $26,630 in 2002. The middle 50 percent earned between $20,800 and $33,580. The lowest 10 percent earned less than $16,530, while the top 10 percent earned more than $41,660.

Salaried agents usually enjoy standard employer-paid benefits that self-employed agents must provide for themselves. Among agencies, those focusing on corporate sales pay higher salaries and provide more extensive benefits, on average, than do those that focus on leisure sales. When they travel for personal reasons, agents usually get reduced rates for transportation and accommodations. In addition, agents sometimes take "familiarization" trips, at no cost to themselves, to learn about various vacation sites. These benefits attract many people to this occupation.

Earnings of travel agents who own their agencies depend primarily on commissions from travel-related bookings and service fees they charge clients. Often it takes time to acquire a sufficient number of clients to have adequate earnings, so it is not unusual for new self-employed agents to have low earnings. Established agents may have lower earnings during economic downturns.

The Downsides

Many travel agents relate that one downside of this career is that they don't have enough free time to do all of the traveling that they would like to do. They are often tied to their desks, especially during peak travel periods such as the summer or important busy holidays. A newcomer would get to take at least one week of vacation a year, more once they've gained some seniority.

The work can also be frustrating at times. Customers might not always know what they want, or their plans can change, and, as a result, the travel agent might have to cancel or reroute destinations that had already been set. There are times when things go wrong, such as severe weather, causing travelers to miss flights, or a member of the traveling party becomes ill and a trip must be canceled at the last minute.

For More Information

Several organizations can provide additional information about careers in the insurance, real estate, and travel industries.

Insurance Sales

General occupational information about insurance agents and brokers is available from the home office of many life and casualty insurance companies. Additional information on state licensing requirements may be obtained from the department of insurance at any state capital.

For information about insurance sales careers in independent agencies and brokerages, contact:

National Association of Professional Insurance Agents
400 North Washington Street
Alexandria, VA 22314
www.pianet.com

For information about professional designation programs, contact:

National Alliance for Insurance Education and Research
3630 North Hills Drive
Austin, TX 78731
www.scic.com

Society of Chartered Property and Casualty Underwriters
720 Providence Road
Malvern, PA 19355
www.cpcusociety.org

Real Estate Sales

Details on licensing requirements for real estate agents, brokers, and appraisers are available from most local real estate and appraiser organizations or from the state real estate commission or board.

For more information about opportunities in real estate sales, contact:

National Association of Realtors
30700 Russell Ranch Road
Westlake Village, CA 91362
www.realtor.com

Information on careers and licensing and certification requirements in real estate appraising is available from:

American Society of Appraisers
555 Herndon Parkway, Suite 125
Herndon, VA 20170
www.appraisers.org

Appraisal Institute
550 West Van Buren Street, Suite 1000
Chicago, IL 60607
www.appraisalinstitute.org

Travel Sales

Information on sales careers in the travel industry can be obtained from:

American Society of Travel Agents (ASTA)
1101 King Street, Suite 200
Alexandria, VA 22314
www.astanet.com

Association of Retail Travel Agents (ARTA)
73 White Bridge Road, Box 238
Nashville, TN 37205
www.artaonline.com

Institute of Certified Travel Agents
The Travel Institute
148 Linden Street, Suite 305
Wellesley, MA 02482
www.icta.com

CHAPTER SIX

Careers in Marketing and Advertising

We grew up founding our dreams on the infinite promise of American advertising. I still believe that one can learn to play the piano by mail and that mud will give you a perfect complexion.
—Zelda Fitzgerald

HELP WANTED: Marketing Project Developer. The headquarters of a nonprofit corporation engaged in providing occupational skills and educational opportunities to employees of a large manufacturing facility seeks a qualified individual to take on a variety of administrative and educational projects. The position requires a high degree of initiative and excellent problem-solving, communication, and writing skills. The successful applicant will have a college degree, perhaps a master's degree, in marketing, project management, or a related field, and excellent computer skills. Competitive salary commensurate with experience. Excellent benefits.

Is the above ad of interest to you? Would you enjoy helping companies determine what the needs and desires of the public really are? If so, consider a career in marketing or advertising.

Defining What Marketing Professionals Do

Well before the sales team hits the road with its merchandise or services, another team of professionals—product developers and marketing, advertising, public relations, and publicity experts—must perform its duties first. The goal of marketing is to reach the consumer—to motivate or persuade a potential buyer; to sell a product, service, idea, or cause; to gain political support; or to influence public opinion.

The fundamental objective of any firm is to market its products or services profitably. To do so, an overall marketing policy must be established, including product development, market research, market strategies, sales approaches, advertising outlets, promotion possibilities, and effective pricing and packaging.

Marketing managers develop the firm's detailed marketing strategy. With the help of subordinates, including product development managers and market research managers, they determine the demand for products and services offered by the firm and its competitors. In addition, they identify potential markets, such as business firms, wholesalers, retailers, government agencies, or the general public.

Marketing managers develop pricing strategy with an eye toward maximizing the firm's share of the market and its profits while ensuring customer satisfaction. In collaboration with sales, product development, and other managers, they monitor trends that indicate the need for new products and services and oversee product development. Marketing managers work with advertising and promotion managers to promote the firm's products and services and to attract potential users.

In small firms, the owner or chief executive officer might assume all advertising, promotions, marketing, sales, and public relations responsibilities. In large firms that offer numerous products and services nationally or even worldwide, an executive vice president directs these activities, which are then coordinated by individual managers.

The Role of the Marketer

In simple terms, salespeople try to encourage customers to buy what they are selling, and marketers try to figure out what the consumers need. Marketers start at the beginning of the cycle, looking at the customer and speculating, "I wonder what they need." Once that need is determined, marketers look at their company and ask themselves, "Do we know how to produce it and can we make money doing it?"

The Steps Involved

Once marketers come up with a product idea—the ideas might come from talking to customers or as the result of brainstorming sessions—they start communicating with the product development department, which in some industries might consist of scientists or engineers. They form a team that includes marketing management, marketing researchers, engineers, advertisers, a financial advisor, and eventually salespeople.

First the team must decide whether the product idea is something that customers really want. This process involves conducting market research. Market researchers develop focus groups, bringing a group of consumers together and talking to them, finding out what isn't working in their present environment and what they truly need.

Professionals working in market research departments are tuned in to the consumer—what he or she worries about, desires, thinks, believes, and holds dear. Market researchers conduct surveys or one-on-one interviews, utilize existing research, test consumer reactions to new products or advertising copy, track sales figures and buying trends, and become overall experts on consumer behavior. Agency research departments can design questionnaires or other methods of studying groups of people, implement the surveys, and interpret the results. Sometimes research departments hire an outside market research firm to handle this task. For example, a market researcher could come up with a procedure to test the public's reaction to a television commercial then turn it over to the outside firm to put the procedure into action.

Marketing research assistants report directly to a research executive and are responsible for compiling and interpreting data and monitoring the progress of research projects.

Once the market research is complete, marketers attempt to quantify that need in the marketplace. If thirty people have told them they need a particular device, that suggests a strong need, but the company can't afford to build something for just thirty people. It wants to make sure there are enough people out there who are willing to buy the product. This sparks another round of research.

With successful research results, the concept-development stage begins. This is the development of a word or paragraph that describes the product. In some instances, marketers then take that concept to engineers or product designers, who develop a prototype of the product.

The prototype is taken to the marketplace for testing and evaluations. With feedback in hand, the team begins to make product improvements.

Once the company is at least 95 percent sure this is the product it wants, it gives the product a final test in the marketplace. The company also tests for claims. For example, a company might want to claim that its new hospital bed will prevent skin sores, but it needs to be able to document that claim.

If all test results point to being able to move forward, the engineers start figuring out how to mass produce the product, and the marketers plan how the company can make money on it. For that, they have to look at the production cost and how much customers would be willing to pay for it. A misconception in this area is that a profit percentage is simply added to the production cost, resulting in the selling price. In reality, prices are determined by knowing what people are willing to pay.

The next step is promotion planning. Now that the company has a product, it has to find a way to get the word out. The appropriate team members make brochures and design advertising.

At the same time, the numbers are being crunched and production schedules are set up. Marketing experts need to know how fast the product can be made, how quickly it can be offered to the public, how many will likely be bought, and how large the profit will be.

Once a date is set for introducing the product, the sales force is brought in and taught how to present it. Then the product is monitored to see whether it is meeting its sale projections. If it is not, management wants to know why and what is going to be done about it. Often, though, if it is meeting or exceeding expectations, management still wants to know why. That's the way it goes in this competitive business.

Where the Jobs Are

Marketing professionals are found in virtually every industry, including motor vehicle dealers, printing and publishing firms, department stores, computer and data processing services firms, management and public relations firms, and advertising agencies.

Because marketers and advertising professionals work hand in hand, many marketing departments are located within corporate advertising departments or within private advertising agencies. Private marketing firms function similarly to advertising agencies and work toward the same goals—identifying and targeting specific audiences that will be receptive to specific products, services, or ideas.

Experts advise looking for an internship before you approach graduation. Those who arrange internships have an edge; they've already become familiar faces on the job. When an opening comes up, a known commodity, someone who performed well during the internship, is likely to be chosen over an unknown one.

Learn as much as you can about the agency or firm you're interested in. In other words, target your prospects.

Working Conditions

Marketers work long hours, often including evenings and weekends. Working under pressure is unavoidable as schedules change, problems arise, and deadlines and goals must be met.

Marketing managers meet frequently with other managers; some meet with the public and with government officials. Substantial travel may be involved. For example, attendance at meetings sponsored by associations or industries is often mandatory.

The Downsides

Although marketing is considered by many to be a step up from sales, there's a downside to it. If the company is not making the expected profit, marketers could easily lose their jobs. Their responsibilities for sales volume and profit are the same as those for salespeople.

In essence, marketers make an agreement with sales departments and personnel. For example, they think, 'OK, we are going to sell a hundred units of X product to a particular customer.' But if they spend too much money in product development or advertising and then sell only ninety units, though the salesperson has the first responsibility, the marketing people are also responsible. Because the marketers and the sales staff had agreed on what could be sold through a specific level of advertising and at a certain price, if the mark is missed, it's the marketers' jobs that are also on the line.

Another downside is that marketers usually supervise salespeople, but the sales force often makes more money than the marketers do—possibly a lot more money. To make up for that disparity, however, marketers usually also receive a good pension plan and bonuses.

Qualifications and Training

A wide range of educational backgrounds is suitable for entry into marketing jobs, but many employers prefer those with experience in related occupations plus a broad liberal arts background. A bachelor's degree in sociology, psychology, literature, journalism, or philosophy, among other subjects, is acceptable. However, requirements vary, depending upon the particular job.

Some employers prefer a bachelor's or master's degree in business administration with an emphasis on marketing. Courses in business law, economics, accounting, finance, mathematics, and statistics are advantageous. In highly technical industries, such as computer and electronics manufacturing, a bachelor's degree in engineering or science, combined with a master's degree in business administration, is preferred.

Courses in management and completion of an internship while in school are highly recommended. Familiarity with word processing and database applications also is important for many positions. Computer skills are vital because marketing, product promotion, and advertising on the Internet are increasingly common. The ability to communicate in a foreign language may open up employment opportunities in many rapidly growing areas throughout the country, especially in cities with large Spanish-speaking populations.

Those interested in becoming marketing managers should be mature, creative, highly motivated, resistant to stress, flexible, and decisive. The ability to communicate persuasively, both orally and in writing, with other managers, staff, and the public is vital. These managers also need tact, good judgment, and exceptional ability to establish and maintain effective personal relationships with supervisory and professional staff members and client firms.

Getting Ahead

Because of the importance and high visibility of their jobs, marketing managers often are prime candidates for advancement to the highest ranks. Well-trained, experienced, successful managers may be promoted to higher positions in their own or other firms. Some become top executives. Managers with extensive experience and sufficient capital even open their own businesses.

Most marketing management positions are filled by promoting experienced staff or related professional personnel. For example, many managers are former sales representatives, purchasing agents, buyers, or specialists in product development, advertising, promotions, or public relations. In small firms, where the number of positions is limited, advancement to a management position usually comes slowly. In large firms, promotion may occur more quickly.

Although experience, ability, and leadership are emphasized for promotion, advancement can be accelerated by participation in management training programs often conducted by large firms. Many firms also provide their employees with continuing education opportunities, either in-house or at local colleges and universities, and encourage employee participation in seminars and conferences, often provided by professional societies.

In collaboration with colleges and universities, numerous marketing and related associations sponsor national or local management training programs. Course subjects include brand and product management, international marketing, sales management evaluation, telemarketing, direct sales, interactive marketing, promotion, marketing communication, market research, organizational communication, and data processing systems procedures and management. Many firms pay all or part of the cost for those who successfully complete courses.

Some associations offer certification programs for these managers. Certification—a sign of competence and achievement in this field—is particularly important in a competitive job market. For example, Sales and Marketing Executives International offers a management certification program based on education and job performance.

Compensation

According to a National Association of Colleges and Employers survey, starting salaries for marketing majors graduating in 2003 averaged $34,038.

Salary levels vary substantially, depending upon the level of managerial responsibility, length of service, education, firm size, location, and industry. For example, manufacturing firms usually pay marketing managers higher salaries than do nonmanufacturing firms. In addition, many managers earn bonuses equal to 10 percent or more of their salaries.

Median annual earnings for marketing managers in 2002 were $78,250. Earnings ranged from less than $30,310 for the lowest 10 percent to more than $145,600 for the highest 10 percent of marketing and sales managers.

Median annual earnings in the industries employing the largest numbers of marketing managers in 2002 were as follows:

Computer systems design and related services	$96,440
Management of companies and enterprises	$90,750
Depository credit intermediation (accepting deposits and lending funds from those deposits)	$65,960

Defining What Advertising Professionals Do

"What's in your wallet?" "Don't leave home without it." "Can you hear me now?" Such phrases are familiar to most of us because of the effective work of advertising specialists. Some consider this phenomenon a nuisance that interrupts television programming and encourages people to buy products that they may or may not really need. Others look upon it as a great public service. A dominating force in our society, mass-media advertising is a multimillion-dollar industry dating back to the invention of movable type in the mid-1400s.

Advertising Agencies

Virtually every type of business makes use of advertising in some form, often through the services of an advertising agency. Companies often look to advertising as a way to boost sales by increasing the public's exposure to a product.

Most companies do not have staff with the necessary skills or experience to create effective advertisements. In addition, many advertising campaigns are temporary, so employers would have difficulty maintaining their own advertising staff. Instead, companies commonly solicit bids from ad agencies to develop advertising for them. Next, ad agencies offering their services to the company often make presentations. The real work for ad agencies begins when they win an account. Various departments within an agency—such as creative, production, media, and research—work together to meet the client's goal of increasing sales.

There are forty-seven thousand advertising and public relations establishments in the United States. About four out of ten write copy and prepare artwork, graphics, and other creative work and then place the resulting ads on television, radio, or the Internet or in periodicals, newspapers, or other advertising media. Within the industry, only these full-service establishments are known as advertising agencies. Many of the largest advertising agencies are international, with a substantial proportion of their revenue coming from abroad.

Most advertising firms specialize in a particular market niche. Some companies produce and solicit outdoor advertising, such as billboards and electric displays. Others place ads in buses, subways, taxis, airports, and bus terminals. A small number of firms produce aerial advertising, while others distribute circulars, handbills, and free samples.

Groups within agencies have been created to serve their clients' electronic advertising needs on the Internet. Online advertisements link users from one website to a company's or product's website, where new product announcements, contests, and product catalogs appear and from which purchases may be made.

Some firms are not involved in the creation of ads at all; instead, they sell advertising time or space on radio and television stations or in publications. Because these firms do not produce advertising, their staffs are mostly sales workers.

Agency Staff

The work at each agency is frequently divided among several individuals or departments—usually including the following:

- **Account executives** make sure that work is completed satisfactorily and on time and to the client's satisfaction. Account executives must be savvy about their agencies and aware of each client's desires and needs. Their responsibilities lie more in the business arena than in the creative aspects of the business.
- **Art directors** must be able to effectively present a theme or idea in convincing visual form through illustration, color, photography, or cinematography.
- **Creative directors** supervise all employees and oversee all activities in the agency. At the top of the hierarchy, creative directors must, of course, be creative and possess people skills and solid business acumen.
- **Researchers** seek to determine what kind of audience would be interested in a particular product or service, why people are interested in the product, and how the public is reacting to advertising campaigns already in place.
- **Media people** work in the department that ensures that commercials are aired on radio and television and that ads get into magazines and newspapers.

Other advertising positions include television producers, print production managers, graphic artists, illustrators, freelance writers, photographers, print production personnel, and traffic managers.

Advertising Copywriters

Advertising copywriters are the real creative force behind ad campaigns. They are the ones who dream up the words for commercials and advertisements and conjure themes for advertising campaigns. Copywriters may also be responsible for developing sales promotion materials, public relations items, billboards, promotional brochures, and articles about products or services.

Copywriters usually begin their work by meeting with the client and/or account executive. After gathering as much information as possible, they let their imaginations flow while looking for a slant on why a product or service is different from all others of its kind. Then they proceed to launch a new advertising campaign with their innovative ideas.

Qualifications and Training

Most entry-level professional and managerial positions in advertising and public relations services require a bachelor's degree, preferably with broad liberal arts exposure.

Beginners in advertising usually enter the industry in the account management or media department. Occasionally, entry-level positions are available in the market research or creative departments of an agency, but these positions usually require some experience. Completing an advertising-related internship while in school provides an advantage when applying for an entry-level position; in fact, internships are becoming a necessary step to obtaining permanent employment. In addition to an internship, courses in marketing, psychology, accounting, statistics, and creative design can help prepare potential entrants for careers in this field.

Assistant account executive, the entry-level account management position in most firms, requires a bachelor's degree in marketing or advertising. At some agencies, a master's degree in business administration may be required.

Bachelor's degrees are not required for entry-level positions in the creative department. Assistant art directors usually need at least a two-year degree from an art or design school. Although assistant copywriters do not need a degree, obtaining one helps to develop the superior communication skills and abilities required for this job.

Assistant media planner or assistant media buyer are also good entry-level positions, but almost always require a bachelor's degree, preferably with a major in marketing or advertising. Experienced applicants who possess at least a master's degree usually fill research positions. Often, they have a background in marketing or statistics and years of experience. Requirements for support services and administrative positions depend on the job and vary from firm to firm.

Since copywriters deal with a wide cross section of ideas and concepts, a general liberal arts background in combination with business is particularly valued. Courses in such subjects as economics, history, journalism, marketing, advertising, math, social sciences, speech, literature, business administration, human relations, and creative writing are recommended.

Copywriters need the skills that all writers should have—the ability to produce clear, concise prose. Therefore, gaining writing experience—in the form of published articles; participation in school, church, or yearbook publications; or internships with local newspapers or radio or television studios—is worthwhile.

Candidates should prepare a portfolio containing at least three ads from two or three previous advertising campaigns. These can be class assignments or real ads from actual clients. If you have no advertising experience at all, present potential employers with samples of your published writing.

Getting Ahead

Success in progressively responsible staff assignments usually leads to advancement to supervisory positions. As workers climb the organizational ladder, broad vision and planning skills become extremely important.

Another way to get to the top in this industry is to open one's own firm. In spite of the difficulty and high failure rate, many find starting their own business to be personally and financially rewarding. Among the self-employed, advancement takes the form of increasing the size and strength of the company.

Employees in advertising and public relations services should have good people skills, common sense, creativity, communication skills, and problem-solving ability. Foreign language skills have always been important for those wanting to work abroad for domestic firms or to represent foreign firms domestically. However, these skills are increasingly vital to reach linguistic minorities in U.S. cities such as Los Angeles, New York, Miami, Houston, and Phoenix.

New media, such as the Internet, are creating opportunities to market products but are also increasing the need for additional training for those already employed. Keeping pace with technology is fundamental to success in the industry. Besides staying abreast of new technology, advertisers must keep in tune with the changing values, cultures, and fashions of the nation.

Compensation

There is a considerable range of salaries in this field, particularly in different regions of the country. The median annual salary in advertising agencies is about $43,000. Junior copywriters may start out earning as little as $25,000; writers with senior status may earn close to $100,000 and even more as creative directors.

The larger the agency or account, the higher the salary will be. The best locations for jobs are in large cities such as New York, Chicago, Detroit, Boston, Atlanta, Dallas, Minneapolis, Los Angeles, Toronto, and Vancouver.

Words from the Pros

Following are the accounts of three professionals in this field. Read on to see whether these careers interest you.

Edward Pitkoff, Marketing and Advertising Professional

Edward Pitkoff of Omaha, Nebraska, attended the Philadelphia Museum School of Art, the Pennsylvania Academy of Fine Arts, Temple University, and Studio School of Art and Design, all in Philadelphia. He also attended a wide variety of marketing and advertising seminars and the School of Visual Arts in New York for a course in television production and direction. He has held several high-ranking positions in marketing, advertising, and sales and is founder and president of Creative Decisions of New York.

"My career began in 1961," says Edward. "After twelve years in positions of designer, assistant art director, art director, and creative director, a freelance business presented itself and I formed Ed Pitkoff Studios, which expanded and evolved into Creative Decisions in 1973, and there the story truly started."

Edward was attracted to the idea of producing high-quality creative advertising that could persuade a consumer to purchase a product. He credits a mentor who taught him to "marry the communication to the consumer so that the buyer could visualize themselves as part of the product."

Edward's advice to those interested in this field involves focus. "Don't ever become distracted," he says. "Always keep your focus on the business of advertising. And remember, what you might want to say to sell this product or service really isn't important. The only thing that is important is what would be compelling to the consumers. What do they want to hear? What do they want to buy?

"Ultimately, it is the consumers who judge how well your message has come across. If the product sells, then you know your focused communication has reached its audience."

Dennis Abelson, Marketing and Advertising Professional

Dennis Abelson earned a bachelor of arts degree in classical languages from Washington University in St. Louis, Missouri, and a master of science in journalism and advertising from Northwestern University's Medill School of Communications in Evanston, Illinois. He has experience as a copywriter, associate creative director, and creative director.

Dennis was working as a freelance writer, but he grew tired of the isolation and wanted more lucrative creative challenges. He was approached by someone who had seen one of his promotional mailings, and together they started a full-service marketing, consulting, and communications firm. After a slow start, the company began to grow and become more successful. Dennis and his partner were ultimately able to disassociate themselves from a third partner and changed the corporate name to Matrix Partners.

The company provides services such as packaging, advertising, promotion, direct mail, and sales presentations. Their clients include a distributor of computer cabling and networking systems, an agricultural biotechnology company, a manufacturer of diving equipment, and several food vendors.

"I originally got into the creative end of advertising because I couldn't see myself holding down a nine-to-five job," Dennis says. "It also gave me the opportunity to keep pursuing my interests in audio engineering and cartooning. In my undergraduate years, I was program director of the campus radio station as well as the creator of a weekly comic strip in the campus paper."

While Dennis says that there is not a typical day in his business, an average day might include revising ad copy, attending project status meetings; finalizing ad copy and sending to the client, reviewing logo designs for new account, performing an online trademark search for a proposed line, eating lunch while working on a presentation, taking calls from clients, working with designers and writers on projects, editing presentations, and writing a direct mailer. Dennis's day would end at about 11:00 P.M.

"What does it mean to be doing my kind of work?" asks Dennis. "At times it seems totally thankless, but in what other profession do you get paid to legally hallucinate, to play creatively with concepts and pictures?"

Among the upsides of his work, Dennis lists a lack of corporate politics or hidden agendas, the opportunity to gain knowledge about many different industries, and the satisfaction of contributing to the success of a client's business.

On the other hand, the downsides include the long hours, difficult clients, and logistical and budgetary constraints on creativity.

Dennis offers this advice about his career: "I would tell others who are considering a career in advertising and marketing to start with the largest organization that will hire you. And be prepared for the long haul."

Jane Ward, Marketing Professional

Jane Ward received a bachelor of arts degree from Catholic University in Washington, D.C. She majored in English, with minors in French and philosophy, and subsequently earned a master of philosophy degree (Irish literature major) from Trinity College in Dublin, Ireland.

When Jane returned to the United States in 1995, she had difficulty finding a job because she had little work experience. She learned Web publishing and ultimately found a job with a good salary. Unfortunately, she found the work boring and began to look for more interesting work. In the interim, she was promoted twice at the Web publishing job.

"When a job as a marketing specialist came up at a software company, it was a perfect fit," Jane says. "I had proven that I could learn technical aspects of a job, and I was able to provide my employers with some writing samples. So since 1997, I have been creating public relations and marketing materials for that software company. I now hold the position of senior marketing specialist."

Jane writes website content and manages the site by supervising the graphic designers and approving graphics for the site. She is responsible for press releases and ad copy and supervises the production of the company's ads. In addition, Jane attends six or seven trade shows a year, staffing the company's booth or speaking to the press about the company.

"I work about fifty hours each week," Jane says. "And since I recently switched from a PC to a laptop, I have been able to bring work home with me. This is both good and bad, I've found. It provides convenience, but sometimes I feel as if work has invaded my home life too much.

"I'm very busy, but the work environment is pretty relaxed, with a very deliberate casualness. In software, people often wear very casual clothes and look down on typical corporate types who wear suits and work in the big city. Also, software, as an industry, is still very young. This is evidenced by the fact that the average age of people working for my company is probably less than thirty years."

Jane describes what she most likes and dislikes about her work. "I enjoy writing something, a press release for example, and then seeing that it was picked up and published by a magazine. It gives me a thrill to see such immediate results of my work. But I don't like going to trade shows because I don't enjoy traveling and having to spend time away from my family. Also, they can get pretty tedious. However, I do understand that it's important for our company to be seen at important shows."

Jane has some specific advice for anyone interested in her line of work. She says, "To individuals who are considering this type of career, I would say learn how to start looking at the world around you with a critical eye. When an ad comes on television, pay attention to it. What was the goal of the people who created it? Who is the target market? What elements did they pull together to create the ad?

"Since I am involved in the writing end of marketing, I would recommend that you learn how to write truly well. I've seen so many college graduates—even those of Ivy League schools—who can't write a complete sentence. And I strongly recommend a liberal arts education, which teaches you how to think and how to articulate your thoughts. These are the kinds of tools that you need to achieve success in any industry."

....

For More Information

The following professional associations can aid in your job search. Many of the publications these organizations produce are available in public libraries.

The American Marketing Association is a professional society of marketing and market research executives, sales and promotion managers, advertising specialists, academics, and others interested in marketing. It fosters research; sponsors seminars, conferences, and student marketing clubs; and provides a placement service. It also offers a certification program for marketing managers. The organization publishes the *Journal of Marketing*, *Journal of Marketing Research*, *Journal of Health Care Marketing*, and an international membership directory. For more information, write to:

American Marketing Association
311 South Wacker Drive, Suite 5800
Chicago, IL 60606
www.marketingpower.com

Members of the National Council for Marketing and Public Relations are communications specialists working within community, technical, and junior colleges in areas including alumni, community, government, media, and public relations as well as marketing, publications, and special events.

The council works to foster improved relations between two-year colleges and their communities throughout the United States and Canada. The association holds an annual conference with exhibits, national surveys, and needs assessments. It also publishes a journal called *Counsel*. Additional information can be obtained by contacting:

National Council for Marketing and Public Relations
PO Box 336039
Greeley, CO 80633
www.ncmpr.org

Sales and Marketing Executives International offers a management certification program. For more information, contact:

Sales and Marketing Executives International
PO Box 1390
Sumas, WA 98295
www.smei.org

CHAPTER SEVEN

Careers in Public Relations and Fund-Raising

*Publicity is the life of this culture—in so far as
without publicity capitalism could not survive—
and at the same time publicity is its dream.*
—John Berger

HELP WANTED: Manager of Communications and Public
Relations. You will manage internal and external communications and public relations activities and implement special
events and projects. You will also work with media and vendors, maintain a presence on the Internet, measure effective-
ness of programs, and direct the writing of press releases,
brochures, public service announcements, newsletters, and
flyers. At least five to eight years of experience in public
relations and communications is required, along with strong
interpersonal and analytical skills and proven writing abilities. Bachelor's degree in communications, journalism, or
public relations required.

oes this want ad inspire any career interest? Many extroverts
feel that their calling is to work in the fields of public relations or fund-raising.

Defining What Public Relations Professionals Do

You might be surprised to learn that the concept of public relations is definitely not a new invention. It dates back to 1787, during the time of the Constitutional Convention. And in the 1800s, both the North and the South made use of the media during the Civil War in an attempt to persuade the populace to adopt their way of thinking.

The goal of public relations remains the same—to sway the public in a particular direction or to build, maintain, and promote positive relationships between two factions: the agencies (or companies) and the public.

An organization's reputation, profitability, and even its continued existence can depend on the degree to which its targeted "publics" support its goals and policies. Public relations specialists, also referred to as communications specialists and media specialists, serve as advocates for businesses, nonprofit associations, universities, hospitals, and other organizations. As managers recognize the growing importance of good public relations to the success of their organizations, they increasingly rely on public relations specialists for advice on the strategy and policy of such programs.

Informing the general public, interest groups, and stockholders of an organization's policies, activities, and accomplishments is an important part of a public relations specialist's job. The work also involves keeping management aware of public attitudes and the concerns of the many groups and organizations with which they must deal.

Public Relations Work

The work of a public relations practitioner falls into six main categories:

1. **Research.** This includes all of the preliminary work that is undertaken to determine the client's goals so that a plan to achieve them can be devised. Library and Internet research, client interviews, surveys, opinion polls, and data collection are all part of this.
2. **Program work.** Once research is completed, a plan is set up based upon the findings.
3. **Writing and editing.** This may include press releases, presentations to clients, internal memos, reports, and magazine articles.
4. **Special events.** Included in this category are press conferences, special appearances, and autograph signings. All are carefully orchestrated to gain the greatest amount of attention.
5. **Media placement.** It is important to select the most important information to release, choose a good time to release it, and send it to the most advantageous receivers.
6. **Fund-raising.** Fund-raising is what sustains nonprofit organizations. Possible events include membership drives, direct solicitations, and benefit banquets.

Those who work as generalists in the field must be able to perform a wide array of duties at the same time. On any given week they may write press releases for one client, design a brochure for another, approach an editor for a third, meet with a talk show host for a fourth, implement a promotion for a fifth, set up a press conference for a sixth, put together a press kit for a seventh, work out the beginnings of a client contact for an eighth, and field media questions for a ninth!

In the government arena, public relations specialists may be called press secretaries, communications specialists, or information officers. A senator's press secretary informs the elected official's constituents of his or her accomplishments and responds to questions from the media and the press. The press secretary schedules and appears at press conferences and issues statements from his or her superior.

Qualifications and Training for Public Relations Professionals

There are no defined standards for entry into a public relations career. A college degree combined with public relations experience, usually gained through an internship, is considered excellent preparation for public relations work; in fact, internships are becoming vital to obtaining employment. The ability to communicate effectively is essential. Many entry-level public relations specialists have a college major in public relations, journalism, advertising, or communication.

Some firms seek college graduates who have worked in electronic or print journalism. Other employers seek applicants with demonstrated communication skills and training or experience in a field related to the firm's business—information technology, health, science, engineering, sales, or finance, for example.

Many colleges and universities offer bachelor's and postsecondary degrees in public relations, usually in a journalism or communications department. In addition, many other colleges offer at least one course in this field. A common public relations sequence includes courses in public relations principles and techniques; public relations management and administration, including organizational development; writing, emphasizing news releases, proposals, annual reports, scripts, speeches, and related items; visual communications, including desktop publishing and computer graphics; and research, emphasizing social science research and survey design, implementation, and analysis. Courses in advertising, journalism, business administration, finance, political science, psychology, sociology, and creative writing also are helpful. Specialties are offered in public relations for business, government, and nonprofit organizations.

Many colleges help students gain part-time internships in public relations that provide valuable experience and training. The U.S. armed forces also can be an excellent place to gain training and experience. Membership in local chapters of the Public Relations Student Society of America (affiliated with the national Public Relations Society of America) or the International Association of Business Communicators provides an opportunity for students to exchange views with public relations specialists and to make professional contacts that may help them find a job in the field. A portfolio of published articles, television or radio programs, slide presentations, and other work is an asset in finding a job. Writing for a school publication or television or radio station provides valuable experience and material for one's portfolio.

Creativity, initiative, good judgment, and the ability to express thoughts clearly and simply are essential. Decision-making, problem-solving, and research skills also are important. People who choose public relations as a career need an outgoing personality, self-confidence, an understanding of human psychology, and an enthusiasm for motivating people. They should be competitive yet able to function as part of a team. It's also important to be open to new ideas.

Some organizations, particularly those with large public relations staffs, have formal training programs for new employees. In smaller organizations, new employees work under the guidance of experienced staff members. Beginners often maintain files of material about company activities, scan newspapers and magazines for appropriate articles to clip, and assemble information for speeches and pamphlets. They also may answer calls from the press and public, work on invitation lists and details for press conferences, or escort visitors and clients. After gaining experience, they write news releases, speeches, and articles for publication or design and carry out public relations programs. Public relations specialists in smaller firms usually get all-around experience, whereas those in larger firms tend to be more specialized.

Getting Ahead

Promotion to supervisory jobs may come as public relations specialists show that they can handle more demanding assignments. In public relations firms, a beginner might be hired as a research assistant or account coordinator and be promoted to account executive, senior account executive, account manager, and, eventually, vice president. A similar career path is followed in corporate public relations, although the titles may differ. Some experienced public relations specialists start their own consulting firms.

The Public Relations Society of America accredits public relations specialists who have at least five years of experience in the field and have passed a comprehensive six-hour examination (five hours written, one hour oral).

The International Association of Business Communicators also has an accreditation program for professionals in the communication field, including public relations specialists. Those who meet all the requirements of the program earn the Accredited Business Communicator (ABC) designation. Candidates must have at least five years of experience in a communication field and pass a written and oral examination. They also must submit a portfolio of work samples demonstrating involvement in a range of communication projects and a thorough understanding of communication planning.

Employers may consider professional recognition through accreditation a sign of competence in this field, which could be especially helpful in a competitive job market.

Compensation for Public Relations Professionals

Median annual earnings for salaried public relations specialists were $41,710 in 2002. The middle 50 percent earned between $31,300 and $56,180; the lowest 10 percent earned less than $24,240, and the top 10 percent earned more than $75,100. Median annual earnings in the industries employing the largest numbers of public relations specialists in 2002 were as follows:

Advertising and related services	$48,070
Local government	$42,000
Business, professional, labor, political, and similar organizations	$39,330
Colleges, universities, and professional schools	$36,820

According to a joint survey conducted by the International Association of Business Communicators and the Public Relations Society of America, the median annual income for a public relations specialist was $66,800 in 2002.

Defining What Fund-Raisers Do

Help Wanted: Director of Resource Development. Seeking an experienced fund-raising professional with demonstrated success with private and corporate foundations and major-donor development; exceptional oral and written communication; solid research, planning, and grant-writing skills; strong relationship-development skills; solid business, goal-driven, results orientation; dynamic personality; initiative and a creative approach to resource development.

As this want ad illustrates, fund-raisers are directly involved in planning and organizing programs designed to raise money for colleges; hospitals; political campaigns; and educational, cultural, historical, community, religious, arts, social service, health, advocacy, political, trade, scientific, and research organizations. Also included are youth leadership and other charitable causes. Sometimes referred to as philanthropy, this industry ranks as one of the ten largest in the United States.

Fund-raisers are usually asked to determine the length and scope of the campaign, slogans or other phrases associated with the effort, how funds will be solicited, and who will carry out these tasks. Then they oversee the efforts to make sure things stay on schedule and go according to plan. They regularly assess and reassess the campaign to determine what changes may be needed.

With enthusiasm, energy, and competence, fund-raisers combine the skills of financial management, public relations, marketing, accounting, human resources, personnel management, and media communications. Assessing the viability of charitable programs, they devise strategies for meeting goals, identify potential donors, and solicit funds effectively. In the 1990s alone, Americans contributed more than $100 trillion to education, health, research, arts, religious, and social welfare organizations.

Fund-raisers may be known as any of the following:

- Director of Major Donor Development
- Director of Annual Giving
- Director of Major Gifts
- Development Director
- Director of Development
- Vice President for Development
- Sponsorship Director
- Director of Resource Development
- Fund-Raising CEO
- Fund-Raising Coordinator
- Fund-Raising Researcher
- Membership Director
- Development Research Coordinator
- Fund-Raising Director of Development

Job Settings for Fund-Raisers

Fund-raisers fall into one of three general categories. The first group consists of staff members in health centers, social services agencies, community groups, nonprofit organizations, and cultural institutions. In each case, they plan and work on all fund-raising projects. For instance, a fund-raiser who is employed by a college may write to large corporations to solicit contributions.

The second group of fund-raisers works for fund-raising consulting firms. These individuals provide advice to nonprofit organizations about the best ways to raise money and manage the funds they accumulate. For instance, a hospital or clinic that is interested in raising money might hire the services of a fund-raising consultant.

The third group of fund-raisers works for companies that specialize in offering fund-raising events for any organization that wishes to raise money. This, for instance, might include carnivals, concerts, and theater parties.

Fund-raisers often work in temporary locations. They constantly attend meetings, present talks, and meet with volunteers. As the campaign progresses, tension grows and the pace becomes increasingly hectic. With the stress of meeting financial goals within a limited time period, fund-raisers often need to work long hours—perhaps seven day weeks—in order to meet the designated goals.

Qualifications and Training for Fund-Raisers

Most fund-raisers have liberal arts degrees, though the degree specialty will vary, and different organizations may require specific qualifications. If you know in advance that you wish to do fund-raising for an environmental concern, for example, then it would be best to focus on a degree in something related, such as environmental studies.

Marketing degrees are also helpful, as is practical knowledge from courses such as mathematics, economics, bookkeeping, and accounting. Other suggested courses include: psychology, speech, sociology, public relations, social work, education, journalism, and business administration.

Individuals considering entering this line of work should have strong communication and numerical skills and be well organized and flexible. They must be able to work well with others and under pressure to meet deadlines. They must be able writers, motivators, and salespeople. Fund-raisers may use special software, such as donor tracking programs, in their work as well as word processing, spreadsheet, and database programs.

Most employers seek individuals with two to seven years of experience. Internships and volunteer opportunities are ways to get experience, and nonprofits have many more volunteer opportunities than business or government jobs. With five years of experience—paid or unpaid—you may choose to become certified by the Association of Fundraising Professionals.

Compensation for Fund-Raisers

Earnings for fund-raisers range from volunteers who work for nothing to those who earn a high income, perhaps $200,000 per year. Earnings vary according to the size of the organization, whether it is nonprofit or for-profit, geographical location, and years of experience. Here are some average yearly salaries:

Entry-level fund-raiser director	$35,000
Program manager	$48,000
Senior-level director	$51,833
Consultant	$75,000
Median overall salary	$52,000

Qualified fund-raisers are in high demand. Since the federal government has cut spending in social programs, the burden of charitable activity has been thrust upon philanthropic sources.

Words from the Pros

Four public relations and fund-raising professionals share their stories to help you see whether these careers are right for you.

Tracy Larrua, Senior Account Executive

Tracy Larrua has more than twenty years of experience in public relations, marketing, and advertising. She attended a performing arts high school, then entered business college, but she ended up working at an advertising agency instead of getting her degree.

Tracy quickly worked her way up the ladder in advertising after six years as an account executive with Ogilvie and Mather. She then began working in public relations, where she has stayed ever since.

In her native Hawaii, Tracy was the owner of TL Promotes, prior to relocating to Los Angeles in 1992. She is active in the culinary, visual, and music arts arenas, and she currently represents musicians, artists, and a production company.

"My typical day is spent writing pitch letters, developing story ideas for editors, and adding, deleting, and updating our media database to be as up-to-date as possible as to what is going on with our clients," says Tracy.

"While wearing a headset, I also make a lot of phone calls. The atmosphere is never relaxed. Actually, it is usually very high stress, but it's a fun stress.

"Our typical work week is forty-plus hours, but depending on client demand, workload, and editorial deadlines, it can easily turn into a sixty-plus week."

Tracy has some advice for anyone considering a career in public relations. "I would recommend that others who are interested in entering this profession get in on the ground floor and act like a sponge. Soak up everything you can," she stresses. "As you start developing your skills, you'll find yourself ascending. Also, stay flexible. This industry has gone through all sorts of changes. Learn, adapt, and adopt a fearless attitude."

Tracy also adds a word of caution. "If you aren't the 'people type,' don't even consider getting into this business. You have to be comfortable and persuasive in talking to people—all kinds of people. Remember, your personality skills count for a lot in this industry."

Betsy Nichol, Public Relations Business Owner

Betsy Nichol heads her own public relations agency, Nichol & Company of New York. She earned a bachelor's degree in journalism from Boston University and has continued to enhance her credentials through seminars and professional workshops.

Like many public relations specialists, Betsy began her career as a journalist. She served a three-month internship at Fairchild Publications and ultimately held a full-time position at its publication, *Home Furnishings Daily*. After three years, Betsy was recruited by a small public relations firm.

"Early on in my career," Betsy says, "someone told me I should have my own business, and at the time I thought he was crazy, but as the years went by I realized that I'm one of those people who is better at being my own boss than working for someone else."

Betsy's initial attraction to the field of public relations was its fast pace and varied responsibilities. She was interested in meeting people from different professions and having the opportunity to learn about many different subjects.

"I also like to communicate in writing," says Betsy, "and good writing skills are essential in the PR business. There's never a dull moment in this business, and being successful requires many of the same skills as being a journalist. It's been an exciting journey.

"Being head of a public relations firm is very hectic," Nichol stresses. "The phone is always ringing, and you never know if it's a client with a crisis, an editor on a deadline, or an employee with a question."

As head of the agency, Betsy spends a good deal of time in meetings with clients or consulting with them by telephone. She also meets with employees to discuss their progress on various projects. In addition, she attends to new business, keeps up with industry standards, and monitors her company accordingly.

To accomplish all of this, Betsy continually monitors her e-mail, talks on the phone, gives instructions to staff, and sends and reviews faxes, notes, and mail that require her attention.

Networking is also an important part of Betsy's career. She attends and speaks at several meetings, workshops, and other events that can lead to new business, provide insight into industry trends, and allow her to form alliances that enable her to better serve her clients.

Betsy talks about the ups and downs of her profession. "The public relations business offers endless ways to express one's creativity. It also demands that one thinks strategically to help clients solve their problems, which keeps me on my toes and makes every day action packed.

"In running a business of twelve people, there is also a great sense of teamwork and caring among the staffers—not a typical office environment. The interaction between us produces exciting results and great fun. The downside is that we often have to cancel evening plans and work late to meet breaking deadlines."

Betsy Nichol offers a suggestion to those interested in public relations. "My advice to others who are considering this field is to work hard and be flexible and both patient and impatient in your quest for success."

Joanne Levine, Public Relations Professional and Business Owner

Joanne Levine owns Chicago-based Lekas & Levine Public Relations, Inc., which specializes in pursuing media publicity for small and midsized businesses.

Joanne did not enter the field in the usual way. She majored in English in college but did not have any ambition to focus on public relations. She joined local community groups while raising her children, and this became a stepping-stone to her future career. While setting up a fund-raising event for one of the organizations, Joanne worked with a public relations professional on the publicity committee. She learned a lot from the experience and became fascinated by the work.

"At the same time, my very creative brother was writing music, forming bands, and starting wacky side businesses," Joanne says.

"One of his companies created and marketed original adult board games he designed. To test my newfound skills, each time he introduced a game, I sent out press releases to the media. The first game, Danger Island, even included me as one of the characters. When the reporters arrived, I became part of the story. We got spectacular local and national coverage.

"That first project really whet my appetite. From there, I began publicizing my husband's retail stores, more civic groups, and the like. One day, I thought about the fact that I was doing a great job and not getting paid for it. I recruited my brother's wife to help me, and we wrote a press release about two sisters-in-law who started a public relations company devoted to small businesses. We got an immediate response from the local chain of newspapers. They wrote a feature article about our company, even though we had no clients. The rest, they say, is history. From that initial article, the phone began to ring, and within a month or two, we had five clients. It's been word of mouth ever since."

Joanne describes media public relations as popular among clients but stressful for the PR professional. In addition to writing copy for brochures and planning special events, Joanne estimates that 80 percent of her time is spent helping to get her clients into newspapers, magazines, and trade publications, as well as on television and radio. Media publicity increases a client's visibility and adds credibility to a client's reputation.

Despite the appeal of media publicity to clients, it is not as popular among the public relations professionals who must do the work. As Joanne says, "With an ad, you know what day it will appear, what size it will be, and exactly what it will say. With an article, I hold my breath until the client and I read it in the publication. With a taped interview on radio or television, I wait to see if anything was cut or taken out of context. While my press release and phone conversation with an editor might have been chock-full of the kind of information I hope they will relay to the public, there are no guarantees, such as those in advertising. I work with editors and writers who are always on deadline, always over-worked, but nevertheless always looking for a good angle. For these reasons, my job can be stressful and sometimes plagued with problems that are completely out of my control."

Despite the pressure, Joanne finds that the positive aspects of her work outweigh the negative. "When all goes well, there's nothing like it," she says. "I have seen the positive results of good, steady media campaigns time and time again. And more than once in a while, a really big media appearance can make an overnight difference in someone's business. The client is on cloud nine, his or her phones begin to ring off the hook with new business, and I am showered with praise and gratitude. I often get to know my clients well and enjoy friendly, upbeat working relationships with them. The knowledge that I am helping to make a client's business grow is very rewarding."

Based on her experience, Joanne Levine offers some practical advice for aspiring public relations specialists. "If you want a career in media publicity, I would advise you to read, read, read," she says. "Study the format of newspapers, watch the twelve, five, six, and ten o'clock news. Read every magazine you can get your hands on and note how things are laid out. Reporters have certain 'beats,' and if you can zero in on what they write about, half the battle is won. Familiarizing oneself with the media is a never-ending responsibility. While there are a few good media guides that provide information, this is not a substitute for studying the style of an individual person, section, or publication. Also, as the media faces the same cutbacks and consolidations as any other industry, frequent changes in personnel happen at a rapid pace.

"If you don't want to go through the trial-and-error process as much as I did, try to get an internship with a PR company. I have used graduate students from the Medill School of Journalism at Northwestern University as freelancers several times. Just remember that in order to make it in this field, you need a good imagination and the ability to find an 'angle.'

"I can't tell you how many times a client has said, 'I do a better job than anyone else in town and I truly care about my customers.' That's very nice, but it's boring! Find out why the client does a better job. What does he or she do differently? Is the business owner an interesting person? What are his or her hobbies? The list goes on and on. You must be able to pick someone's brain until something newsworthy pops out. Then you must learn who might be fascinated with your information, so much so that they want to inform their readers about it or share it with their television audience."

Thomas L. Campbell, Director of Development and Alumni Relations

Thomas Campbell earned his bachelor's degree in business administration in 1981 and a master's degree in physical education in 1987 from the University of Delaware. He also received a master's degree in business administration from Wilkes University in 1990. He is a Certified Fund Raising Executive (National Society of Fund Raising Executives) and serves as director of development and alumni relations at Allentown College of St. Francis de Sales in Center Valley, Pennsylvania.

Thomas's career at Allentown began almost by accident. In 1988 he was interested in relocating to Pennsylvania from Florida and looked upon his interview at Allentown College as good practice. He was offered the job, which he decided to accept and keep for a few years before moving on. Thomas has stayed with the job since that time because he loves it.

"Since I had always worked in sales, the work involved was really not that dissimilar," Thomas says. "I found that fund-raising was just another version of sales but with a wonderful twist. The work was now impacting students' lives. I know that without the money I raise, many of our students just wouldn't be able to attend college. And since I recognize the value of a college education and the impact it can have on someone's life, I am very motivated to do this kind of work."

Since fund-raising can be a complex job, Thomas says that his work days are usually different. As he says, "There are no days that are 'typical.' The overriding object is to raise money, of course, but there are lots of steps. You just don't call someone up and expect them to give you money. It's all about relationship building, cultivating people, and identifying potential donors."

For Thomas, the job has more positive than negative aspects. He says, "This kind of work brings much joy and is very fulfilling. I would say that the most difficult aspect of this position is that it is sometimes difficult to rise to the challenge of exceeding the previous year's performance."

Thomas Campbell offers some advice for anyone considering a career in fund-raising. "I would advise others who are interested in entering this career to first secure another type of job on the corporate side. With that kind of experience to your credit, you are a much stronger fund-raiser because you understand what executives must deal with and what they are up against."

For More Information

For information on careers in public relations, see the listings for the American Marketing Association and the National Council for Marketing and Public Relations, listed at the end of Chapter 6.

Information about careers in fund-raising may be obtained by contacting:

Association of Fundraising Professionals
1101 King Street, Suite 700
Alexandria, VA 22314
www.afpnet.org

Association for Healthcare Philanthropy
313 Park Avenue, Suite 400
Falls Church, VA 22046
www.ahp.org

Direct Marketing Fund Raisers Association
224 Seventh Street
Garden City, NY 11530
www.dmfa.org

About the Author

J an Goldberg's love for the printed page began well before her second birthday. Regular visits to the book bindery where her grandfather worked produced a magic combination of sights and smells that she carries with her to this day.

Childhood was filled with composing poems and stories, reading books, and playing library. Elementary and high school included an assortment of contributions to school newspapers. While a full-time college student, Goldberg wrote extensively as part of her job responsibilities in the College of Business Administration at Roosevelt University in Chicago. After receiving a degree in elementary education, she was able to extend her love of reading and writing to her students.

Goldberg has written extensively in the occupations area for *Career World Magazine*, as well as for the many career publications produced by CASS Communications. She has also contributed to a number of projects for educational publishers, including Free Spirit Publishing, Capstone Publishing, Publications International, Scott Foresman, Addison-Wesley, and Camp Fire Boys and Girls.

As a feature writer, Goldberg's work has appeared in *Parenting*, *Today's Chicago Woman*, *Opportunity Magazine*, *Chicago Parent*, *Correspondent*, *Successful Student*, *Complete Woman*, *North Shore Magazine*, and the Pioneer Press newspapers. In all, she has published more than three hundred pieces as a full-time freelance writer.

In addition to *Careers for Extroverts and Other Gregarious Types*, she is the author of fifteen other career books published by McGraw-Hill.